FEDERMAN FRENZY

f^ede_rMan fren_zy

the **cult** in culture
the **me** in memory
    the **he** in his _story

Encounters with Raymond Federman

cameliaelias
editor

Federman Frenzy: the cult in culture, the me in memory, the he in history
Encounters with Raymond Federman

Copyright © EyeCorner Press 2008
Published by EyeCorner Press 2008
Edited, designed, and typeset by Camelia Elias

ISBN: 978-87-992456-4-2

A version of this book was published by Aalborg University, Dept. of Language and Culture. Open source web text.
Research News Nr. 1. General editor: Bent Sørensen

All rights reserved.
No part of this book may be reproduced in any form, without written permission from the publisher.

Denmark
www.eyecorner.press

We all overlap within the twofold vibration of history.

– RAYMOND FEDERMAN

CONTENTS

CAMELIA ELIAS
Take It, Leave It, Fold It:
Playing with Raymond Federman 9

LISBETH RIESHØJ AMOS
Noodling Around:
on a frame-breaking [de]tour through Federman's surfictions 17

JESPER CHRISTENSEN
Hypothetical Reality:
Federman's Narrative Strategy 35

BENT SØRENSEN
Second Thoughts:
Federman's Cultural and Individual Memory
in The Twofold Vibration 49

CAMELIA ELIAS
Sesame Undone:
Negotiations of Virtual Space
in Federman's blog [the laugh that laughs at the laugh....] 63

CAMELIA ELIAS & RAYMOND FEDERMAN
Epilog[ical] Encounters 93

TAKE IT, LEAVE IT, FOLD IT
Playing with Raymond Federman

CAMELIA ELIAS

TO WRITE would be first of all TO QUOTE. The writer would not be the one who listens to a voice from within, but rather the one who quotes, who puts language into quotes, who both sets if off and calls it to himself, who in a word, designates it as language.

— Federman, *Critifiction*

We are on the threshold of celebrating writer Raymond Federman's 80th birthday. Those familiar with Federman's writings will agree with us that this is a gift in itself, especially since Federman is still prolific and writes prose, poetry, and criticism that is as interesting as in his early experimental days that go back to the 60s. If one knows Federman well, however, one will grant us that he gets better and better. Federman himself would concur.

While the present publication is not intended as a *Festschrift* as such – although any writing on Federman can be considered a celebration in itself – it aims to introduce the reader to aspects in Federman's writing that have become classics. However, insofar as these concepts are dynamic, they can be said to produce fresh, relevant, engaging, and at times personally involved readings. In other words, Federman at 80 keeps it simple and urges us on to consider what is important.

What one discovers in Federman's simplicity is first and foremost a desire to be generous. What is important to him is to give readers an experience that they can really think about. With this mindset he thus wants to appeal to all readers, if given the chance. Which brings me to introducing the first keyword that concerns his writings: chance. It is by pure chance that he survived the Holocaust after his whole family died in the concentration camps; it is by pure accident that he became a professor of literature; and it is by pure hazard that he became a writer of variations over the same theme: his loss, and what might have happened. In the face of death, obviously nothing would have happened. As he did not participate in the collective act of dying, his first responsibility towards the ones who have become memories – whom he also refers to as "the potentials" when he does not render them graphically as four Xes, XXXX – was to then turn to writing and say something exactly about potential.

But Federman did this in a somewhat inverse order. As it is not him who chose the event of death to put into words, he would look at how words elected him to say something about it, yet under the mark of potentiality. He would ask himself questions that go like this: how was it possible that a French Jew who came to America in the 40s turned writer because he found words "sexy"? He would often provided an immediate answer, which can be rendered like this: words found him "sexy" in turn. The fact that he found a symmetrical relation between word and writer on a seductive level gave Federman a ground onto which he could consolidate his position as a writer vis-à-vis the stories that inspired or informed his own existence. As the story goes now in his own words, he is "a fucking good writer." Above all stories, *this* is the story of his life, and he sticks with it.

What I find priceless in Federman's writing is the fact that not only does he invent new categorical terms that we can use to think about the space of literature – such as *critifiction* (for bridging criticism and creativity), *surfiction* (for bridging the now and tomorrow, or the man and his morrow, as one might also put it) and *precipice* (for bridging gaps and gallows) – but he also plays with literature in the very sense of the word. He always banks on creativity and he is never afraid that it might go bankrupt. If one bears in mind that chance has potential inherent in it, then the ground for playing games is laid. Thus Federman plays games, creates games, gambles with words, and invites his readers to consider the meaning of winning streaks through writing. Insofar as his premise always rests on the commonsensical fact that playing games is more fun than frustration, his writings suggest that there is no way in which even the saddest event could not be rendered in terms that elicit a lot of laughter, especially if written about in the context of the ludic.

His writings are always populated with the strangest characters, who do and say the most hilarious things about the most serious things. They talk a lot, reveal a lot about themselves and the world in which they live, and they are always clever enough to recognize the world for what it is: a place where originality is embedded in "pla(y)giarizing." If one were to describe Federman in one word, one would have to say, fun. Federman's biggest insight is that any creative act that involves the making of the game in the image of the other requires a double play that relies on the invitation to take it or leave it. Playing the other by copying the other's moves is what enables Federman to raise metaphors and idiomatic expressions such as "take or leave it" and "double or nothing" to their indexical value. In a game you can't show too much, but you can talk incessantly. Thus these expressions get the privilege to title Federman's books. In their certainty – it's either this or that – such titles have the function to destabilize the hesitant reader, but ultimately they always win her over.

Where I find Federman most generous is in his trusting the reader to go with him – and learn. What one learns are lessons such as these, for example, from *Double or Nothing*: "That's the problem with talking too much. Eventually you reveal yourself. But when you don't talk you become a suspiciously suspicious character."

In the present volume four talkers attempt to undo the "suspiciously suspicious character" with view to grounding Federman's work in its own desired floating and flight from the merely consistently brilliant, phenomenal, and always clever writing. Federman's idea is that any writing should have a solid dose of banality in it, lest it should get too high on its horse.

The four essays have their own histories. All four spring from a workshop panel on haunted writing at a conference in Karlstad that Bent Sørensen and I organized some years ago. We had invited two of our students to participate as well, who have since completed their educations with most brilliant theses either on the man himself, Federman, or on postmodern topics that take their point of departure in some of Federman's theory and key concepts, particularly critifiction. We set some rules in advance. The demand was – as any good game goes – that if we should fail to impress the people in the audience, then perhaps we should devise instead a method of haunting them thereafter. The reader will soon discover for herself which self-imposed task the essays have managed to accomplish best in their own individual way: to haunt, silence, seduce, prophesy the future, or in truly Federmanesque fashion, fuck it all up.

As we all, however, have had a good master in Federman, the strength of this volume is to be found in its reflecting a tight proximity between the reader (of Federman) and the writer (on Federman). But every good thing comes at a price. What we have paid in our aim to achieve this proximity is a whole lot of inescapable overlapping. The reader here will discover that we all tend to quote the same Federman books or other same texts, but as far as we are concerned, this overlapping as a palimpsest of chance is something we have welcomed. In fact the last two essays in the volume have more consciously played with using the same texts in order to test precisely the validity and value of variation against the background of haunted writing. When one thinks of haunting in general terms, if the ghost is identified, then it is so not because of its ability to stir variation, but rather its ability to create the same (just think of the motif of the *doppelgänger*).

In this sense, the angles and takes on Federman here are thus different and hopefully revealing of precisely that combination between the banal and the brilliant that Federman himself was so good at both creating and keeping in check. The first essay (Amos) takes the reader through Federman's narrative strategies of concrete prose and frame-breaking, and the second (Christensen) picks up the narrative strategy thread through a discussion of hypothesis. The third (Sørensen) can be said to introduce the notion of culture through strategic and hypothetical memory, while the fourth (Elias) takes potentiality through stages of the immemorial that are informed by conjuring laughter at the gates of dawn. Here the operative demand, "Open Sesame!" is articulated through the mouths of virtual agents in cyberspace. This last essay is also longer than the others. There is a reason for that. While the ideas expressed rely on formulations articulated at the Karlstad conference, the aim now is to show how such ideas can be transposed into a world where the ghost is not only in the book, but also in blogging, on the Internet machine. So we can be twice as haunted, twice as vibrated.

The volume ends with an *inédit* surprise in the form of an epilogue that shows Federman at his best: when he cares for his readers, and when he instructs them by allowing them to actively participate in the intellectual game in which the established rules are those meant to show that personal history is only as extravagant as we turn it into. The epilogue is an exchange between Federman and myself on a private basis. I was invited last year to give a talk at Babes-Bolyai University in Cluj, where the topic was on the first person plural narrators in Federman's fiction. Before I presented my draft, I shared it with Federman who offered in return a most astonishing piece of text.

This text, while highly personal, and thus very moving in its thrust, shows Federman's generosity and concern with his readers. I say 'moving,' because this exchange was not motivated by any interests. Federman solicited my writing, and in return he gave me his thoughts. Although his thoughts flattered me, they were not offered to merely flatter. As it happens, Federman knows what my position is on praise whose purpose is to validate and endorse. I care for neither validation, nor endorsement. I care for open curiosity that goes places.

Federman graced me with his. On a general level, what is also illuminating and thoroughly life-affirming is the fact that, although 80, Federman is still genuinely interested in what position he occupies in the literary historical tradition. Granted, he has moved on from questions regarding his status as an experimental, postmodernist writer, as hilariously illustrated in this line from *Aunt Rachel's Fur*:

> I was sad to see postmodernism disappear before we could explain it, I kind of liked postmodernism, I was happy in the postmodern condition, as happy if not happier than the previous condition. I don't remember what that was called but I was glad to get out of it (245).

Yet the sense that one gets from Federman's personal missive is that he sees the notion of exchanging ideas as the most significant act in the continual formation of any one writer or reader, be they 40 or 80. As a gesture of courtesy – and perhaps paying for disappointing Federman for having edited his email to me where he makes statements as to the 'sexiness' of my writing – I returned the favor and wrote a prose poem in honor of two of his most interesting characters, Moinous and Namredef. Me & Us and Federman backwards paying tribute to what in writing constitutes the highest stage of creativity: appropriating, pla(y)giarizing, quoting the xs, "the potentials," and listening to their voices as they designate language *in absentia*:

x x x x

The patient reader will thus be rewarded with a full blown critifictional autobiography where the lives and times of Federman and Elias are entangled in the key to astonishment.

Roskilde, May 15, 2008

NOODLING AROUND
on a frame-breaking [de]tour through Federman's surfictions

LISBETH RIESHØJ AMOS

It's a great story, I hope you're not in a hurry, because it's going to be a long detour, but essential, wait till you hear...

— Federman, *Aunt Rachel's Fur*

The Jewish writer and critic Raymond Federman was born in France in 1928 and immigrated to the United States of America in 1947. During World War II, when Federman was still only a boy, his parents and two sisters were deported to Auschwitz and exterminated there. Federman only miraculously escaped death because his mother pushed him into a closet before his family was taken away. These traumatic memories form the underlying story of all Federman's literature.

With his two highly experimental novels *Double or Nothing* (1971) and *Take It or Leave It* (1976), Federman presents us with two somewhat thinly disguised versions of his autobiography while, at the same time, he explores the problematic concept of representation. With their pronounced emphasis on the actual process of production, playful displacement of words on the page, and high level of self-reflexiveness, these novels can be classified as 'historiographic (radical) metafiction.'

The purpose of this essay is to investigate some of the narrative strategies employed by Federman, in particular his use of different types of frame-breaking techniques, including concrete prose, which foreground one of the most central issues in Federman's fiction: the (im)possibility of finding an appropriate linguistic representation of autobiographical experiences. This essay argues that Federman's pronounced use of metafictional strategies is perhaps the most adequate approach for him, if he is to at least *attempt* to recover and confront the unspeakable memories of his past.

Intrusive Commentary:
putting the past under erasure

The fictional writer who interferes with the story he is telling to such extent that it never actually gets told is a frame-breaking strategy that is frequently employed in Federman's novels. Using such strategies inevitably foregrounds the process of production, the telling of the story, or in Federman's case, the impossibility of telling the story. *Double or Nothing* and *Take It or Leave It* are both examples of novels that dramatise the struggling writer in his desperate attempt at rearticulating a past of unspeakable events. In both novels, Federman presents us with numerous key autobiographical elements around which his narrators constantly interweave layer upon layer of digressions and interrogations in their attempt to understand and recover the historical truth.

What is interesting though is the manner in which Federman's narrators deliberately play down the whole theme of Jewishness and the Holocaust. The teller in *Double or Nothing*, for example, insists that "this is not [...] a Jewish story" (Federman, 1971: 40), and similarly the second-hand teller of *Take It or Leave It* claims that "[I don't want to insist too much on the Jewish side of this story but one cannot avoid it altogether I just hope you guys don't make too much out of it]" (Federman, 1976: 223[1]) – the latter statement is even literally bracketed off from the rest of the discourse by Federman's own square brackets. Despite such overt claims, it becomes clear that both narrators cannot drop the subject entirely, as it is repeatedly, almost compulsively, alluded to throughout their discourses. This is explicitly manifested in *Double or Nothing* where the main teller struggles with the articulation of an appropriate opening for his story (Federman, 1971: 42). Below, two texts in facsimile from page 48.

```
No past
The Statue of Liberty
Nothing before the boat
All that crap about the War the Farm the Camp the Lampshades excluded
You start just like that on the boat
```

---

[1] My pagination, which will be used henceforth as regards all quotations taken from *Take It or Leave It*.

```
Nothing
 beyond
    the
   boat                                   I
                                           mean
                                              nothing
                                                    in
                                                     the
                                                       past
                                                         in
                                                        fact
                                                         the
                                                        whole
                                                        story
                                                           is
                                                            a
                                                        break
                                                with the past
THE WAR         THE CAMPS         THE FARM     !
```

The second-hand storyteller in *Take It or Leave It* uses a similar technique, though in an ironic tone:

> I'm not going to make you weep / o-o / with all the sad stories he told me and yet if I wanted to tell you all the crap he told me (the trains the camps) if I wanted to describe in details and realistically all the misery and suffering he endured (the lampshades the farms the noodles) we would never get out of here / o-o / ah yes his entire family remade into lampshades (father mother sisters ah yes uncles aunts cousins too) you wouldn't believe it (wiped out)! (Federman, 1976: 184).

Calling attention to these traumatic past events only as a means of explicitly stating that they will *not* form part of the discourse, that they "won't come into this story" (Federman, 1971: 135), paradoxically has the opposite effect. These deliberate attempts of cancelling out any elements that can be associated with the Holocaust merely foreground their present absence. Continuously haunting Federman's narrators, the momentary glimpses we do get of the past remain strangely present in the background of the novels. They thus become something that requires, yet simultaneously defies, representation, implying that there is more to these stories than meets the eye, so to speak, but that it can never be successfully seized or recovered by Federman's narrators.

By situating the teller in an extra-diegetic position, Federman not only dramatises but also clearly foregrounds the existential aspect of the imaginative process of production: the idea of reinterpreting and coming to terms with the traumatic experiences of his past through the act of 'storyfication.' Using the frame-breaking strategy of intrusive commentary, Federman creates a realm in which a sense of co-existence between two ontologies is maintained. This allows for a dialogue between the writer and his discourse, as the former goes through the painstaking process of approaching the historical truth by turning it into a story. Never seeking to hide the fact that these autobiographical elements are always introduced within a fictional context, the notion of the teller as the authorial creator of his text remains possible for us to believe in. However, this idea cannot be maintained throughout Federman's two novels, which I want to elaborate on in the following.

Collapsing Worlds:
when fact and fiction become interchangeable

The worlds that Federman creates are by no means simple. They might appear simple at first, but as I want to illustrate now, Federman soon deprives us of any stable centre of orientation, leaving us with worlds that are most suitably described as 'impossible.' Towards the end of both *Double or Nothing* and *Take It or Leave It*, the frame-breaking activities become so radical that "all the rules and regulations are going down the drain" (Federman, 1976: 261). In fact, the only rules that can possibly be applied to these contradictory and highly illogical universes are the 'rules' of fiction.

At the very beginning of *Double or Nothing*, a whole section, paradoxically entitled "THIS IS NOT THE BEGINNING" (Federman, 1971: 0), has been devoted to explaining the four-level narrative hierarchy in which the teller is situated. Ironically, the whole idea of overtly establishing this neatly structured framework is done only in order for it to be playfully broken down again. This meta-section can be attributed to the fourth person who (in a footnote) claims that he is "hidden somewhere in the background omnipresent omnipotent and omniscient to control direct dictate a behaviour to the three other unfortunate beings" (000000000.0). Presumably this voice thus represents the implied author of the text, Federman-the-paper-author, who inhabits the highest level of the narrative hierarchy. Gradually descending within this recursive structure, we find a "middle-aged man" (0) whose task it is to record the activities of yet another man, namely the teller who is to invent the story of the protagonist (with a background conspicuously similar to Federman's). Towards the end of the story, this initial framework is radically undermined, starting with the two lowest levels of the discourse. As the teller claims how "eventually [the protagonist] too would lock himself in a room with noodles to crap out his existence on paper" (124), it becomes evident that the two of them are overlapping. Federman's frame-breaking activities do not stop here but are stretched even further to include all four diegetic levels (below from p. 173).

```
And here we are (the two of us ** the three of us *** the four of us ****)
a year later (let us say) exactly a year after the boat landed in New York
and all of us (I * HE * WE * US) got all excited in the subway because the
girl with the legs spread apart smiled at US and now 365 days later here I
* HE * WE * go again getting all exicted with another female (a much bigge
r one this time) having converged into one another (the protagonist and th
e inventor -- and of course by extension the recorder too) it's unavoidabl
e it had to be
```

Demolishing the foundation on which we rely in order for us to make sense of this discourse, Federman leaves us very little, if any, solid ground against which anything can be verified.

In a similar fashion, the world of *Take It or Leave It* also becomes more and more self-contradictory, as the protagonist, on his way to Camp Drum, all of a sudden addresses his creator, the second-hand teller who (presumably) inhabits a superior world,

> Hey listen! Would you mind if I told this part of the story myself? I mean directly. Because you see now we are coming to the climax, I mean the real juicy part, and it would be better, and also much more suspenseful if I were to speak directly – first-hand!

I don't mind (I told him, when the time comes). But can you pull it off? Can you handle it by yourself? I mean, remember, I am the one who is supposed to recite this tale second-hand. And besides, it is not legal, you know! What will our listeners say when they discover I've handed you the narrative voice?

Please let me try! Just for a while. For this one part. It really means a lot to me! You'll see, I'll do it right!

Okay! (Federman, 1976: 377)

As the second-hand teller passes over the authorial voice, he does in effect recognise himself as a fictional construct and we are therefore no longer able to maintain the notion that he and the protagonist exist on different planes. Leaving the protagonist in charge of the recitation has serious consequences for the framework of the novel, as the telling and the told become somewhat indistinguishable. As the protagonist struggles to keep his Buick Special on the road, this struggle is mirrored in the narration, which is equally difficult for the protagonist to keep on the right track – or is it the other way round? Federman's text offers us no stable frame of reference: we are unable to determine whether this is to be read metaphorically or literally. Both readings seemingly apply, though our logic dictates that we cannot have it both ways. In the end, both journey and narration swerve off course and into a ditch.

Undermining the fictional framework in his novels, Federman removes the solid foundation and textual 'depth' that we normally depend on in order for us to make sense of a text (hence his own classification of these novels as 'surfictions'). Everything within these irrational universes is therefore subsumed by language and, consequently, the tension between historical fact and fiction, memory and imagination, ceases to exist. Thus our experiences from the empirical world no longer suffice as a means of interpreting the universes that Federman creates. The only thing that undoubtedly remains 'real' is the physical existence of the book we are holding in our hands.

Concrete Prose:
an attempt at 'visualising' the unspeakable past

Indeed, the physical existence of his novels is something Federman foregrounds, as *Double or Nothing* and *Take It or Leave It* are highly innovative in their typographical layout. Reading these novels almost equals a visual cinematic experience. We are literally forced to manoeuvre the book around as we encounter numerous textual segments that are printed diagonally across the page, upside-down or sideways, and instances of shaped typography that through their form simulate the shape of real-life objects and processes. In other words, Federman clearly subverts the traditional use of typography and, consequently, the extreme physicality of his typographical designs continually disrupts the projected worlds of his texts. Although the use of concrete prose emphasises the 'bookiness' of Federman's novels and therefore serves as an ironic self-representation, I would argue that employing such strategy should not *merely* be seen as a playful jest. There is, in fact, an inherent sense of doubleness in these novels; a constant vibration between seriousness and playfulness, articulation and disruption, and Federman's use of concrete prose is no exception. This technique too becomes a way of insinuating the serious elements of his past that lie in wait beneath the ludic surface of his discourses.

Page 7.1 of *Double or Nothing* is referred to as "Digression on potatoes" in the "SUMMARY OF THE DISCOURSE" (Federman, 1971: 192) at the very end of the novel (see Plate 1). This page appears as the teller considers whether potatoes or noodles would be the most appropriate food for his one-year seclusion. Having settled on noodles, this page could of course quite literally be seen as a 'digression on potatoes.' However, this is an understatement; a deliberate attempt at disparaging, yet again, the haunting presence of Federman's unspeakable past. The page number too with its ".1" certainly suggests the intentional attempt at turning something highly significant into something insignificant. Here we find the sequence of the four Xes that carefully inscribes the loss of Federman's family as a visible sign. In placing the sign that marks the erasure of his family above a swastika so conspicuously large that our eyes are automatically drawn to it, Federman produces a short segment charged with emotion and painful loss.

Another example in which Federman plays down his Jewish origin can be found in *Take It or Leave It* on page 40 (see plate 2). Here the symbol of Jewishness, the Star of David, stands out remarkably from the page, yet its significance is deliberately denied and mocked by the discourse that forms one of the two triangles constituting the symbol itself, "of course I'm Jewish You guys didn't know Look at my nose But that doesn't mean that I'm some sort of fanatic about all that crap about religion tradition deportation extermination etcetera et" (Federman, 1976: 40). As we have already established, the act of retracting the sudden and reoccurring allusions to "the Jewish side of this story" (223) has the opposite effect. This example points to the fact that Federman cannot completely evade his traumatic past as it haunts the many different levels of his discourse.

The final example of concrete prose that I want to discuss is also taken from *Take It or Leave It*. This textual segment on page 253 (see plate 3) is best described as a 'conceptual icon' and is probably the closest Federman gets to the historical truth: the unspeakable "SYSTEMATIC EXTERMINATION" of his family. Again, the four Xes (here literally introduced only within square brackets) signify the present absence of his obliterated family. The lack of any syntactical continuity and the many gaps between the fragmented words convey a deeply moving visual image of Federman's great loss. This is an image that stays with the reader, remaining visible as an afterimage implanted in the reader's mind long after the book has been read.

Using concrete prose as a narrative strategy, Federman not only foregrounds the materiality of his books, but he also clearly points to the fact that words and the traditionally static arrangement of these simply do not suffice when attempting to capture the unspeakable historical truth. By literally shaping the linguistic material in various ways, Federman creates numerous instances of 'concrete sayings' that work in a twofold manner: we can look at them as pictures *and* we can read them as prose.

However, no matter how we choose to read the many competing discourses that constitute each of his novels, the fact remains that Federman never tries to deceive us: his pronounced use of frame-breaking strategies always points to the fictionality of the few glimpses we get of his traumatic past.

Real Fictitious Discourses:
writing autobiography

> I lurch forward [...] and dive into my story even if that means repeating myself somewhat after all let's be honest a biography or a guy's past experiences it's always something one invents afterwards in fact life is always a kind of fictional discourse a lot of bullshitting! (252)

With these words, the narrator in *Take It or Leave It* captures the essence of what is being practised in Federman's two novels. The frame-breaking strategies, as we have seen, certainly foreground the problematic process of transforming elements of the past into stories. By constantly breaking the fictional framework, Federman leaves us with only allusions to a historical truth that lurks beneath the textual surface, while at the same time, he repeatedly reminds us that these novels are linguistic constructs. The serious issues that haunt Federman's discourses can therefore never be validated as 'solid' historical facts. The overt fictionality of Federman's autobiographical accounts, however, does not mean that he denies the existence of his past. Rather, he clearly acknowledges the past as discursive, thus it can only ever be accessed by means of textuality – always in a mediated form. In *Critifiction: Postmodern Essays*, Federman elaborates on this idea and claims that,

> [F]iction and autobiography are always interchangeable, just as life and fiction, fact and fiction, language and fiction, that is to say history and story are interchangeable. And this because, for me, the STORY always comes first. Or to put it slightly differ-

ently: everything is fiction because everything always begins with language, everything is language. The great silence within us must be decoded into words in order to be and to mean (Federman, 1993: 89).

Double or Nothing and *Take It or Leave It* are clearly manifestations of this paradox: remaining forever unreliable, language is however our only means of *attempting* to approach and make sense of the world around us, past as well as present, although it never allows us to represent or seize the 'real' event. So, when one of Federman's many voices in *Double or Nothing* claims that "you're getting everything confused […] his story and my story" (Federman, 1971: 65), the obvious pun on "history" signifies Federman's own view on the constant and reciprocal interplay between fact and fiction.

References

Federman, Raymond (1971). *Double or Nothing: A Real Fictitious Discourse*. Chicago: The Swallow Press Incorporated.

───── (1976). *Take It or Leave It: an exaggerated second-hand tale to be read aloud either standing or sitting*. Fiction Collective.

───── (1993). *Critifiction: Postmodern Essays*. Albany: State University of New York Press.

McHale, Brian (1999). *Postmodernist Fiction*. London: Routledge.

Rieshøj Amos, Lisbeth (2005) *Surface Disturbances: A Reading of Raymond Federman's Surfictions as Historiographic Radical Metafictions*. Working Papers 39. Aalborg U: Dept. of Languages and Intercultural Studies.

Waugh, Patricia (2001) *Metafiction. The Theory and Practice of Self-Conscious Fiction*. London: Routledge.

```
Yes but the POTATOES    the raw
                POTATOES  on the train (remember?)   what a story:   A
                          on the way to the CAMP                    N
                                       the CAMP (X * X * X * X)     D

                                                                    I

                                                                    F
                                                                    O
                                                                    L
                                                                    L
                                                                    O
                                                                    W
                                                                    E
                                                                    D


                            [swastika]                              M
                                                                    Y

                                                                    S
                                                                    H
                                                                    A
                                                                    D
                                                                    O
                                                                    W

Can't come into this one...Nothing before the boat...

(Damn good story!)  Could sneak the potatoes in...Next time.

The train
The rats
The old man
The farm
The camps
The potatoes... Wow!

                    A TIME OF POTATOES

could have a whole series          like that 20 or 30 volumes
could have a whole series          a kind of Balzacian comedy

                    THE VEGETABLE COMEDY

no even better than that

                    THE HUNGER COMEDY

                                   no even worse than that

                    THE STARVATION COMEDY

                         20 or 30 volumes in folio.
```

PLATE 1

ME! at least I had some education [at the time] <u>Le Certificat
d'Etudes!</u> (In France — *OUI* — Lycée Henry IV) at the beginning
of the war . . . . But after that — *OUI* — a big hole :
ooooooooooooooo
o   o
o   o
ooooooooooooooo   Yes a big H O L E —
        the debacle the occupation
        the Germans the French
        the   J E W S   the

                  o
               f cou
           rse I'm J
      ———————— *ewish You guy* ————————
        — — *s didn't know Loo*— — —
          — *k at my nose But that*— —
          doesn't mean that I'm som
        e sort of fanatic about all t
      hat crap about religion tradition
    deportation extermination etcetera et

        the yellow star & then the great roun-
        dup in 42 (le 14 juillet) the entire fam-
        ily mother father sisters uncles aunts
        cousins everybody picked up every-
        body remade into lampshades (after
        the showers)yes   at AUSCHWITZ!

Ah!   the camps
       the trains
       the farms (in the South)
       the raw potatoes (and diarrhea all night)
       AND I FOLLOWED MY SHADOW [remember
that's what he called it]
Well let's skip all that --
No need to whine about it   That's for sure!
And then AMERICA — that FAT bitch — in 47! in 1947 — in
August!

<><><>< OH DO TELL US THAT STORY AGAIN DO TELL US ><><><>

Ah what a man he was my father (obviously he is reinventing him somewhat) I was thirteen when they picked him up and the rest of the family on that sinister 14 juillet or thereabout with their yellow stars and their cries and their little bundles   my mother was howling down the staircase tears rolling down from her eyes   huge tears   and my two sisters too   and on top of that at thirty my father (Damn did he have a rough life! I wonder why he didn't commit suicide?) he became tuberculous yes twice a week had to have stuff pumped into his pneumothorax   saloperie! sometimes during the night he would start choking and spitting blood   my mother knew what to do but she would panic anyway (at this point Benny and Marilyn started weeping like two kids)   he had eyes gray like a stormy sky my father but my father ∿∿∿∿∿∿∿∿∿∿∿∿∿∿ my father

```
[X - X - X - X]        SYSTEMATIC  EXTERMINATION        [X - X - X - X]
                       ¥ ¥ ¥ ¥ ¥ ¥ ¥ ¥ ¥ ¥ ¥
--------------- de ----------------------- camps ----------- jui --------
------ mè ----------------------- cre ------------------- lam -----------
--------------- savo ------------------------- uillet ----------- Ausch ----
---- tra --------------------- ferme ----------------------- pè -----------
-------------------- bilité ---------------- rat ----- ap ------ ap ------
----------- rès ------------------------ si ------------------- vac ---------
--------------------- mer ----------------------- de -----------------------
```

PLATE 3

HYPOTHETICAL REALITY
Federman's Narrative Strategies

JESPER CHRISTENSEN

The reality of imagination is more real than reality without imagination, and besides reality as such has never really interested anyone, it is and has always been a form of disenchantment. What makes reality fascinating is the imaginary catastrophe that hides behind it.

– Federman, *Critifiction*

Nineteen years old, the French Jew Raymond Federman arrived in America in 1947. Here the young man eventually became a scholar, critic and an accomplished author of experimental literature – what he refers to in his own terminology as 'critifiction' and 'surfiction.' The subject in his literary production is predominantly a self-conscious attempt at writing the life story of this young man, and his writings can best be described as 'historiographic metafiction.' Briefly stated, one might describe Federman's work as greatly inspired by the claustrophobic textual concerns of Beckett, and closely related to Sterne in its preoccupation with how to go about autobiography.

At the core of Federman's writings is the fact that he lost his entire family in the Holocaust. This essay will look closer at the specific narrative strategy of how Federman includes hypothetical notions in his work. The textual examples are taken from Federman's two novels: *Double or Nothing* (1971) and *Take It or Leave It* (1976). Moreover, this undertaking will include an investigation of how these texts deal with the issues of memory and potentiality within the ephemeral framework of historical facts and fate.

Double or Nothing

In 1971 Federman published a novel whose full title is: *Double or Nothing – a real fictitious discourse*. It is a self-cancelling text that is concerned with describing the preparations involved in writing the story of a young man who arrives in America shortly after World War II. Ostensibly this is Federman's autobiographical account. However, throughout the text this presumption becomes increasingly difficult to maintain. An example of this is the narrative stance in the text. The text stipulates that no less than four separate entities are involved: the '*first person*' is the recorder, the one who scribbles the story down; the '*second person*' is the teller of the story who is to spend 365 days confined in a room creating the story; the '*third person*' is the protagonist, who is given different names several times throughout the text, and who has to wait for his life to be written; finally there is the '*fourth person,*' who is the author proper – implicitly Federman – who renounces all claims to authorial responsibility. Indeed, this is an example of how something can be both double *and* nothing. Thus, confusion and self-contradiction are constant throughout the text.

Confronting the Past through Hypothetical Reality

The persistent use of hypothetical notions throughout the text contributes greatly to the unsettling of any grounding in solid fact in the novel. This becomes apparent in the final page of the novel, where a detail in the budget for the planned 365 days writing process is found to be inaccurate:

> IMAGINE THAT! that means that you now have 52 dollars (416 less 364 leaves 52) more to work with ..... and therefore we have to start all over again It's quite obvious: JUST THINK... FOR INSTANCE...IF THE ROOM COSTS ONLY 7 BUCKS A WEEK.. [...] Then it does not necessarily have to be N O O D L E S ! THE END (Federman, 1971: 191).

This is an example of how Federman uses hypothesis to completely cancel out the text in its entirety. The reader is reminded that nothing in the text has been granted the status of being a textual reality: all 191 pages are merely hypothetical mental notions – a suggested textual reality, as it were – of what could be written.

This constitutes a general narrative strategy that reappears in both Federman novels analyzed in this essay: the use of hypothesis as a means of confronting the issues of historical fact. The haunting memory of Federman's exterminated family plays an especially crucial part in this. Throughout *Double or Nothing* there are many allusions to the fate of the protagonist's family. Here is an example:

> [...] of course French Jews don't speak it [Yiddish] any more A dead tongue for them A least [sic] not the new generation the left over generation the reduced generation Those who didn't end up as lampshades (I don't have to go into that but it's there in the background and will always be there Can't avoid it even if you want to THE CAMPS & THE LAMPSHADES (Federman, 1971: 39).

And later on:

> (you can't avoid the facts) But we must forget about that about the Jews the Camps and about the L A M P S H A D E S (never again) (Federman, 1971: 181).

All these passages where the family is mentioned or alluded to are carefully defined as something that will not be mentioned in the text. Thus mentioned in the form of *sous rature*, erased yet still present, the protagonist's family members are painfully conspicuous in their absence, just as the repeated reference to them as x-x-x-x. X is the mathematical sign for the horizontal line, that which is unknown. The etymological origin is the Latin *abscissa*: that which disappears. The implication is that within Federman's self-cancelling hypothetical discourse, the haunting memory of his absent family is granted existence. Only within a discourse in which nothing is real, but merely exist as hypothetical notions, can we be told of the absent family. So absurd and unfathomable is the absence of an entire family that it takes a discourse in which nothing can be certified as being a textual reality proper for Federman to be able to confront this gruesome twist of fate.

In fact Federman expresses a strong wish to dissolve the painful past that lies before his arrival in America. As seen in the two quotes above, Federman attempts to avoid the memories of the haunting past even though he realizes that it is impossible:

> I could use my own name It might get confusing though because people will start identifying me with him that's dangerous must avoid that A Russian name? Originally his father came from Russia but you can't go into that Nothing beyond the boat [from France in 1947] I mean nothing in the past in fact the whole story is a break with the past THE WAR THE CAMPS THE FARM ! THE WAR THE CAMPS THE TRAIN [Cattle transportation train, presumably going to the Auschwitz concentration camp, from which the young Federman escaped] THE FARM Nothing of all that as though he had not even been marked <u>Consciously</u>. Or at least he doesn't know it <u>obviously</u>. I do of course <u>necessarily</u>. That should come in flashes. <u>Images</u> (Federman, 1971: 48–9).

Through the narrative strategy of creating a hypothesis, Federman can establish a textual environment, a zone where the conventional textual reading protocols do not apply. Moreover, by unsettling and displacing any concept of reality, the reader can perhaps begin to comprehend the unutterable tragedy of Federman's past. The memory of X-X-X-X is introduced as that which will not be mentioned. Thus, the use of a predominantly hypothetical discourse allows the erased to re-appear while at the same time leaving the past undisturbed.

The reader is brought into a state of reading where the concept of 'double or nothing' can be grasped. It is an oscillation between historical reality and a potential/hypothetical textual reality – a twofold vibration – from which glimpses and mental images of Federman's memory of his lost family can be grasped. The unutterable remains unsaid, yet the notion of that which has ceased to be remains.

Take It or Leave It

Much like *Double or Nothing*, Federman's 1976 novel *Take It or Leave It* is a circular, self-cancelling text. The narrative stance is complicated somewhat, insofar as the narrator informs us that he was told the story by the protagonist under a tree. As such, the story has passed through several hands – or, more to the point, different memories – before the reader sees the text.

Again the ostensible autobiography revolves around the protagonist, Frenchy (who has a past very similar to Federman's), and his experiences as a paratrooper in the American army. Frenchy is granted a month's paid leave before he is to be shipped overseas to fight in Korea. This time is to be spent sightseeing in America. However, due to a bureaucratic error, the protagonist has to travel some 3-400 miles up near the Canadian border to collect his money. It is on this journey that we travel along with Frenchy, and are told of his past.

When Hypotheses Take Over

> It's not logical . . . fucks up the whole system! Imagine what will happen . . . – what the POTENTIALS will say when they hear about this! (Federman, 1976/1997: 254)

This extract illustrates well the way in which hypothetical mental notions distort the distinction between reality and hypothesis in *Take It or Leave It*. The result is a state of *aporia* where logic ceases to apply as a relative term by which one might gauge what reality is and what hypothesis is within the narrative. This suspends the entire text in limbo. But meaning is still conveyed onto the reader. However, to distinguish between Truth and Hypothesis is a matter of careful deconstruction. And yet, as we shall see below, even this distinction cannot be obtained. For, as the use of hypothesis increases in the novel, it becomes completely impossible to separate such potential instances from actual occurrences. Thus, it really becomes a matter of 'taking it or leaving it.'

This view on reality is further elaborated later on in the text, where a situation in the protagonist's past is described. Upon arriving in America, Frenchy was taken in by an uncle and his wife, and the situation develops into a *ménage à trois:*

> He [Frenchy] was so to speak in a between-time-stage a financial meantime a virtual present rather than a true or actual present not to mention the emotional in-between therefore he was in suspense between two lives and it in this meanwhile this parenthetical gap this temporal spread this existential displacement (Federman, 1976/1997: 222–3).

Again we see how historical time, existential status and truth are replaced within Federman's discourse. Here hypotheses take over to such an extent that no distinctive hegemony of either hypothesis or truth can be established. Such a textual 'zone' of complete *aporia* can also be described as a hypertrophied-hypothesis.[1] When a text enters this level, which lies beyond the principle of reality/hypothesis, a complete surrender to *aporia* must be accepted.

An example of just how complicated or 'perverted'[2] a discourse that is a hypertrophied-hypothesis can be is seen in the following example, where the protagonist tells the following to a narrative entity who suddenly materializes inside the traveling car:

> What do you think I would be today if it were not for Hitler? Do you know what I would be? A tailor! Yes a little Jewish tailor Boulevard des Italiens. Or else an instituteur in some retarded school. But let me assure you I would not be on my way to Camp Drum [to obtain the money for his leave] discovering America. I would not be here with such a nice guy like you making up my life as I go along. No! Certainly not. Therefore funny as it may sound Hitler in a way was my Savior! (Federman, 1976/1997: 263).

We here witness how hypothesis is used to illustrate the arbitrary nature of fate. Through applying a playful stance on potential out-

---

[1] For a complete definition of this concept as well a close examination of the theory on temporal hypotheses, see Christensen, 2004.

[2] Another definition of Federman's text as far as the complicated and oscillating sense of time in a narrative is to describe it as 'perverted,' a term which Gerard Genette used to describe Marcel Proust's *A la recherché du temps perdu*.

comes within the past, the protagonist illustrates how the discourse can distort reality. The comment on how Hitler saved the protagonist from a dull and uneventful life is of course sarcastic, for Hitler was certainly not the saviour of the victims of the Holocaust. Through contrasting the actual contemporary situation with several hypothetical notions of what might have been, the haunting memory of those who fell behind, the x-x-x-x, is again prominent through their absence.

The overall state of *aporia* within the text, which is largely due to the use of hypothesis, is summed up in the following meta-comment on the narrative structure of *Take It or Leave It*:

> It is not easy I tell you for someone who lacks experience and imagination to handle this type of twin situation — situation which brings together elements of the past and of the present on the same level (not to mention elements of the future and of the potential) (Federman, 1976/1997: 296).

Such a 'twin situation' is one that Federman has dealt further with in his 1982 novel, *The Twofold Vibration*, wherein the oscillation between various historical periods of the protagonist's/Federman's life, including future events, occurs. Again, this novel is seen as falling into the category of hypertrophied-hypothesis.

Returning to *Take It or Leave It*, we have established that the distinction between reality and hypothesis is completely insoluble. Towards the end of the novel this becomes apparent to the protagonist. He has traveled along the snowed up, icy road to reach the military base and his money. Suddenly he skids off the road, into the precipice. Luckily a giant tree breaks his fall:

> I waited like that. Hurting all over. For hours. Two. Three Four. I seemed to have lost the notion of time. And in fact I had lost it. And also the notion of space. I was in total nothingness! In complete LESSNESSness my friend Sam would say where nothing is even less than nothing (Federman, 1976/1997: 381–2).

The protagonist thus expresses the textual *aporia* that lies beyond hypertrophied-hypothesis. Just as in the closed space of one of Samuel Beckett's texts, Frenchy/Federman seems to acknowledge that a textual realm can be created in which all dimensions of reality can be dissolved. As Frenchy tells us:

> For in fact, all experience is both active and passive, the unity of the given and even the construed, and the construction one places on what is given can for that matter be either positive or negative. It is what one desires, or fears, or is prepared to accept, or it is not! (Federman, 1976/1997: 210).

For Federman as an author, the realm of *aporia* that can be reached through a continuous use of hypothesis is the perfect setting for dealing with autobiographical memories. When a discourse cannot be definitively validated in terms of historical reality or simply as the Truth, then the personal pain that stems from the haunting memory of the past becomes bearable.

(Un-)remembering the Past

> [...] there was no need to choose: the memory could have been left so far behind that one day its "reality" wouldn't matter any more. Of course it happened. Of course it didn't happen. (Pynchon, Gravity's Rainbow: 667)

Reading Federman's texts is to witness a constant challenge of the conventional relationships between the concepts of both historical facts as well as fictional facts. As Federman cautions at the onset of *Take It or Leave It:*

> All the characters and places in this book are real, they are made of words, therefore any resemblance with anything written (published or unpublished) is purely coincidental (Federman, 1976/1997: Epigraph).

Raymond Federman is a survivor attempting to come to terms with his fate. In his literary production he succeeds in telling the story of himself and his absent family by not telling it. By displacing all discursive grounding in reality through the constant use of mental hypothetical notions, Federman circumnavigates the pitfalls of sentimental representation. The mimetic representation of the past via a textual discourse is an illusion that is successfully dismantled in the novels *Double or Nothing* and *Take It or Leave* It.

In these texts, Federman reminds us that narrative, its space and time, are but constructs. Whether the narrative concerning his family, the x-x-x-x, can be ascertained as either real or hypothetical has ceased to be of importance. By conveying the most painful parts of his narrative through the use of hypothesis, that is, forwarding potential mental notions of history through a discursive *sous rature*, the reader attains a unique empathy for Federman's haunting loss. For, by not telling and explaining the reasons for this reluctance, Federman has successfully surrendered his memories to us. The paradox is that we fully believe in Federman's memories by accepting that we do not know which, if any, part of his historical discourse is truthful. Just as history is a discourse we tend to trust, memory is a discourse which we choose to believe in; much depends on the framework of its representation.

In his comments to Steven Spielberg's movie, *Schindler's List*, Federman expresses his difficulties with watching the historical re-enactment of the Auschwitz concentration camp:

> Me, usually, when watching a movie, I wonder how they do it? How they fool me, how they make me believe that the little boy who just got shot by Goeth is really dead and not faking it. After all I heard the sound of the bullet leave the gun and heard it enter the little boy's skull. I saw the crushed skull, and the blood, even though shown in black & white. I heard that, I saw that. Or was it an illusion? (Federman, 2004).

The point is that the past cannot be recreated. A sensory illusion can never fully create a credible illusion, although it may be ever so effective. As we have seen, Federman's approach to the representation of the past is much more subtle. Yet, in his elusive discourse of the past, Federman succeeds in conveying to the reader a mental sense of his haunting loss.

References

Christensen, Jesper (2004). *Interfictional Pockets – A Narratological Investigation of Temporal Hypotheses and Hypertrophied-Hypothesis in Postmodern Literature.* Working Papers, Nr. 34. Aalborg: Dept. of Languages and Intercultural Studies.

Federman, Raymond (1971). *Double or Nothing.* Chicago: The Swallow Press.

_____ (Ed.) (1975). *Surfiction – Fiction Now... and Tomorrow.* Chicago: The Swallow Press.

_____ (1976/1997). *Take It or Leave It.* FC2, Illinois.

_____ (1981/2000). *The Twofold Vibration.* København: Green Integer.

_____ (1993). *Critifiction.* Albany: State University of New York Press.

_____ (2004). "Notes scribbled in the dark while watching Schindler's List." [http://epc.buffalo.edu/authors/federman/shoes/schindler.html]

Genette, Gérard (1983). *Narrative Discourse – An Essay in Method.* Ithaca: Cornell University Press.

Pynchon, Thomas (1973/2000). *Gravity's Rainbow.* London: Vintage.

SECOND THOUGHTS

Federman's Cultural & Individual Memory in *The Twofold Vibration*

BENT SØRENSEN

> *You have to get on with things, sustain your excessiveness.*
>
> The Twofold Vibration
> – Federman

French born writer and critic Raymond Federman is best known as a practitioner and theorist of experimental fiction and as the inventor of terms such as 'surfiction' and 'critifiction,' both denoting a type of literature where literary theory and practice meet in an acutely self aware form of mythographic metafiction. After coming to the US at the age of 19 in 1947, Federman studied creative writing at Columbia University, wrote a celebrated PhD thesis on Samuel Beckett, and worked for many years as a professor of literature at SUNY, Buffalo. This essay is concerned with the playful representation of memory and history and its consequences in his 1982 novel, *The Twofold Vibration*. The novel poses questions about the intersections between political activism, history, popular culture and memory.

Plot and Narration in *The Twofold Vibration*

The novel sets up a narrative hierarchy which evolves organically as the narrative progresses. At first it seems quite clear that the main narrator, who uses the first person singular to refer to himself, and who is referred to by his (imaginary) interlocutors (or readers) as "Federman," has control over this hierarchy. However the situation soon becomes more complicated, as it turns out that the main protagonist of the novel, known only as "the old man" or "the old guy," shares most or all of the biographical features of "Federman," the narrator. This conflation of personal history is presented as one of the crucial operations of the novel and of the writing of personal as well as general history:

> [This] means that the old man was born in 1918, like my father, coincidentally, or for that matter like me, fictitiously speaking, what's the difference, we are all extensions of one another, the living as well as the dead, we all overlap within the twofold vibration of history (Federman, 1982/2000: 11).

One should not be fooled by the phrase, "fictitiously speaking," since it is paradigmatic within Federman's understanding of writing that it is always "real fictitious," as witnessed by the use of this phrase as the subtitle of his 'novel' *Double or Nothing* (Federman, 1971/1991).

The next operation of conflation of narrators and their status in the system has the potential for moving two ways in the diegetic hierarchy: either one diegetic level up, namely to the 'real' author, Raymond Federman, whose biography one can then examine for similarities with "Federman," the narrator; or one diegetic level down, namely to the protagonist level within the novel.

We shall look first at the protagonist level, where we next encounter "our friends Moinous and Namredef" (Federman, 1982/2000: 23). This pair of characters later grow in importance in the novel, as they are entrusted with more and more powers, eventually becoming substitute narrators, dutifully reporting back to Federman on their endeavours to trace and rescue the old man. Of course, the notion that "we are all extensions of one another" is also applicable to the diegetic status of these two characters, a fact further underscored by their names, which variously reveal them to be "Federman" spelled backwards and a compound of two personal pronouns in French, 'moi' and 'nous' – or, MeWe. They are thus literally extensions of the first person narrator, who conveniently has split his persona into these four agents, allowing him to let any and all of the personae comment on both the others and on the progress of the narrative as such.

Metafictional Jewishness

This radically metafictional technique is not covertly employed by Raymond Federman, but on the contrary pointed out explicitly to the reader. In this quote the notion of Jewishness is also brought into focus:

> oh you people didn't know Namredef and Moinous are Jewish too, well I haven't mentioned it because I thought it was obvious,

and anyway this is not their story, they are incidental here, they have been introduced simply for the convenience of the narrative, to help along, to allow some shifts o point of view and some creative free play (153–154).

The theme of Jewishness has been introduced at a very early stage of the narrative, but its importance has been played down by "Federman," the narrator: "[T]he old man [...] had to struggle all his life to conquer vanity and indolence and [was] of Jewish origin on top of that, not that this fact makes much difference here, not at all, it's quite irrelevant to this story, or barely relevant" (18–19). This statement is belied by the events to unfold later in the narrative, where it turns out that the old man's ethnicity and family's destiny is of highly marked significance.

This is already evident a few pages later, where we casually learn about his parents' and sisters' fate: "His parents were so poor, [...] and did they suffer, their entire lives, from hunger and humiliation, before they were exterminated, and his two sisters too, xxxx out, is how he always put it" (22). The 4 Xes discretely represent the erasure of the four humans constituting the family unit, not only of "the old man," but also of Federman, the author. Thus it is in this nexus of personal memory and history that the conflation of diegetic levels becomes especially evident. The denial of the importance of the Jewish ethnicity is x'ed out by the reality of the Holocaust experienced as re-doubled on both the authorial ("real") and character ("fictitious") levels. Simultaneously, the diegetic levels from author, through 'paper author,' narrator and protagonist/character are thoroughly imbricated, and the difference between them is x'ed out or put *sous rature*.

The re-doubling of character and author's Jewish destiny is quadrupled by Namredef and Moinous's Jewishness, which we have already quoted the revelation of. Immediately preceding that passage, the two characters confess their ethnicity, but deny that it colours their contemporary life – unlike that of "the old man":

> Is it because you're Jewish, asked Namredef totally out of breath, I'm Jewish too and I don't get excited like you when I am in the midst of Germans, you can't blame them all, is it because your entire family was exterminated by the Nazis, so what, mine too was remade into lampshades at Auschwitz, or have you forgotten

> And mine too, mine too, intervened Moinous who was holding on to his side as he trotted along splashing in the rain (153).

"The old man" replies with his own denial of the importance of ethnicity, but interestingly uses a Jewish term of derogation ("schnorrers") to characterise the two characters:

> The old man shrugged his shoulders, It has nothing to do with that, and besides I'm not worked up, I'm just being philosophical, that's all, the two of you always confuse ideology with sentiment, yes it's amazing how you two schnorrers always have to reduce everything to your Jewish sentimentality (153).

Later the reader, as well as all the individual personae, is addressed with a similar term from Yiddish discourse, again denoting mild but playful derogation:

> It's all there, you schmucks, inside the words, teller and told, survivors and victims unified into a single design, if you read the text carefully then you'll see appear before you on the shattered white space the people drawn by the black words, flattened and disseminated on the surface of the paper inside the black ink-blood, that was the challenge, never to speak the reality of the event but to render it concrete into the blackness of the words (225).

At this point the reader must give up believing in the narrative hierarchies, since too much diegetic and thematic conflation has occurred. Each narrating and narrated persona has been revealed as unreliable and double-voiced or double-voicing. The theme of erasure has been countered by the paradox that erasure (into "white space") takes place through the marking (with Xes: "simple design," "black words") of a page, much like the smudging of the pages by the author in the act of writing the novel we are reading.

History and Future Nazism

In her position paper for the subproject on Cities and memory on the ACUME website, Monica Spiridon writes:

> There are many ways of building identities: the starting points, the dimensions, the purposes of the projection and especially the audiences which they address are always different. Yet, all these processes have something in common. *Individuals as*

well as communities have to imagine their identity in relation to some landmarks, selected by the individual and the public perception. These landmarks organize identities along some important lines: to be more specific, they help understand, justify and evaluate – either positively or negatively – their self-perception and the perception of the Other (Spiridon, 2002).

The tension posited here between individual and collective memory is operative in Federman's work. In all memory work he advocates for the place of invention as an empowering tool for both the aesthetic practice of the novelist and the ethical project of the historian.

The truth of whether personal history and memory determines the future life and acts of the personae, or whether all these acts are lived out in the shadow of cultural memory and destiny is thus an issue that presses itself in the foreground more and more as *The Twofold Vibration* progresses. The risk of history playing itself out in a circle game as suggested by the phrase "it's starting all over again" (9) in the novel's first sentence is strongly underlined by the theme of "the space colonies" which "the old man" is waiting to be deported to at the novel's outset. These "space colonies" are a thinly veiled caricature of the death camps of the Nazi's, and the superficially benevolent rhetoric of the government justifying the colonies closely echoes Nazi propaganda:

> [U]ndesirables are sent, you know criminals and perverts, madmen or those who are considered physically or mentally abnormal, social derelicts, the useless ones, the good-for-nothings and others too, isn't it a tremendous idea, old folks and sick people are also sent there, the incurables, that solves the prob-

lem of the aged, social security and medicare, and it also wipes out crime and unemployment, not to mention sexual perversion

artists too are sent there, yes especially experimental artists whose work is found totally unredeemable according to the new idealistic social and aesthetic norms now in vogue (13).

And best of all: "[T]hey make more space for the rest of humanity" (13) i.e. *Lebensraum*. This satire of utopianism as well as belief in efficiency and rationality as tools for controlling history shows Federman's program to be mainly an aesthetic one, but one that never loses sight of the political implications of a given aesthetic stance. This becomes clearer when we return to Federman's non-fiction on the poetics of postmodern metafiction, as well as his personal essays on how and why to be a Jewish writer. What is evident here is that the future is fraught with much the same perils as the past, as history was. We are doomed to repeat our failures if we do not allow space for human invention in both senses of the term.

History, Activism, and Memory

But now we turn to the segments of his novel, *The Twofold Vibration*, which explicitly thematize the issues of history and memory. From the outset we (the readers and the whole coterie of co-narrators being addressed directly) have been told by "Federman," the narrator, that the whole story is a repetition of a previously occurred and told sequence of events: "Hey you guys wake up, it's starting all over again, but this time it's going to be serious, the real story, no more evasions, procrastinations, and you won't believe this, it begins in the future" (9), which further more is told from "a potential point of view, premembering the future rather than remembering the past" (10). Much as history at large repeats itself with the concentration camps re-doubled in the figure of the space colonies, Federman's personal history redoubles itself in the old man: as Federman, the author, escaped deportation to Auschwitz, "the old man" is left behind when the rocket leaves for the space colonies: an excess that nobody even wants to bother with deporting.

Next we zoom in on one of the prememberings referred to above, namely the sequence which begins with "the old man's" involvement in the anti-Vietnam War movement in the USA. "The old man" accidentally becomes embroiled in a campus demonstration in Buffalo, New York, in the late 1960s. He performs what amounts to an *acte gratuite* by hurling a bicycle at a policeman, and from there he becomes propelled by events beyond his control into a role as a political activist/celebrity. The pace picks up when a thinly veiled Jane Fonda-like character, June Fanon, chooses to champion the cause of the "Buffalo 45," of whom "the old man" is cast as a leader by the media. As casually as "the old man" hurled the bicycle, the two 'activists' fall for each other's charms and decide to "forget about the revolution" and elope together to Europe. This apparently irresponsible act is further motivated by "the old man's" assertion that "most of us live our politics in the past" (to which Fanon replies: "Or in the future") (79), and, what is more, that "political understanding is but a series of second thoughts" (68).

Both characters escape the historical moment of the 1960s without qualms: Fonda/Fanon already planning the emotional depths of future film roles that have yet to be created for her (for instance, her Oscar winning performance in 1978 in *Coming Home*); "the old man" dreaming of repeating a fabulous winning streak at the roulette tables of Monte Carlo.

In the greater scheme of the novel, both these pursuits are presented as far more substantial than 1960s counter cultural activism. The couple therefore go on a trip which gradually evolves into a journey of remembrance for "the old man," which takes him from casino tables to the Nazi death camps that are symbolically figured as a birthplace for the character's second, surplus life in America.

Thus the novel's preoccupation with history, remembering and premembering, leads us to present a twofold thesis: "The old man's" accidental political radicalism leads to remembrance of and obsession with the past, which ultimately is redeemed in an effective working through of trauma; whereas Fonda/Fanon's carefully designed, but futile activism leads nowhere but back to Hollywood, simply because it does not result in any exoneration of a past burden or guilt, but merely serves as a future oriented publicity strategy.

Thus, it is in the cross-field between history or cultural, shared memory and individual, personal story that the way forward may be forged, paradoxically of course by moving backward into personal memory. So, despite the eventual declaration that "History is bankrupt" (234), the debts that history cannot meet can be canceled by an individual project of replenishing the coffers of memory. Therefore the project of writing Jewish history remains an impossibility, yet a necessity for the individual Jewish writer. The scale on which this is possible for Federman is captured in the anguish of the following quote: "I am often asked," Federman writes, "as a survivor of the Holocaust and as a writer: 'Federman tell us the story of your survival'. And I can only answer: 'There is no story. My life is the story. Or rather, the story is my life'" (Federman, 2001).

Federman's ability to write of history can only be realized via remembrance as narrative strategy: one writes in order to prevent collective forgetfulness, and remembrance reveals that which is *sous rature*, erased but still legible. "It is necessary to speak," he says, "to write, and keep on speaking and writing (lest we forget) about the Jewish Holocaust during the Nazi period even if words cannot express this monstrous event. It is impossible to speak or write about the Holocaust because words cannot express this monstrous event" (Federman, 2001). We cannot go on telling it, but we must go on.

Personal and Cultural Memory

The final twist in the tale of Federman, the author's, dramatization of his personal fate comes in another quote from the same article, entitled, tellingly "The Impossibility of Being a Jewish Writer":

> Take my case for instance. What do you think I would be today if it were not for Hitler? Do you know what I would be today? I mean if nothing had happened. No war, no occupation, no collaboration, no deportation, no extermination – no Holocaust. Yes, do you know what I would be today? A tailor. A little Jewish tailor slaving in a tailor shop on Boulevard des Italiens in Paris. Or else an instituteur in some intellectually retarded school in the province of France. But let me assure you [and here the protagonist and the author merge into one], I would not be a

writer (an experimental writer, I am told), dealing with such an important topic as the Holocaust. No, I would not be here, making up my life as I go along. Certainly not. Therefore, funny as it may seem, disturbing and grotesque as it may sound, Hitler in a way was my savior. Yes, I know it's laughable, preposterous, but it's true (Federman, 2001).

The paradoxes involved in being created by your greatest destroyer or in the tension between liberation and loss, are echoed in the words of the old man in *The Twofold Vibration*, speaking to Fanon, but in fact narrating his past experiences to us all:

[T]he fact of being a survivor, of living with one's death behind, in a way makes you free, free and irresponsible toward your own end, of course you feel a little guilty while you're surviving because there is this thing about your past, your dead past and all that, but you have to get on with things, sustain your excessiveness (Federman, 1981/2000: 99–100).

Memory sets you free from the yoke of history. History never lets go of the bridles of one's individual memory.

In *Critifiction*, Federman's collection of essays on postmodern literature, he elevates this principle to a general poetics, complete with a cultural criticism that frames the dismissal of Fanon's future strategy, which leads only to the space colonies, or back to the concentration camps:

Until very recently one read novels – especially those written in the first person – as though they were mere autobiographies, and it was assumed that the writer merely wrote what he **re-**

membered of his life, of his youth, of his family, of his amorous adventures. Consequently, **memory** (voluntarily or involuntarily) was considered the sole mechanism that made personal or autobiographical fiction possible [...] Contemporary experimental fiction is no longer written as **remembered events**, but on the basis of **invented events** which seem to be happening (very much as in the cinema right before the reader's eyes, in the present (author's emphasis throughout) (Federman, 1993: 100–101).

This quote, of course, describes Federman's own fictional (or fictitious) practice in novels just such as *The Twofold Vibration*. The twofold-ness of such works lies exactly in the fact that the dynamics between memory and invention is kept in eternal motion, never resting long on one pole.

We thus know very little new about Federman's real life after reading what could be supposed to be an autobiographical account, but we know infinitely more about the function of memory as a strategy for dealing with trauma, loss and guilt, after reading what could equally easily be supposed to be a wholly invented, fictionalized holocaust story.

References

Federman, Raymond (1971/1991). *Double or Nothing: A Real Fictitious Discourse*. Fiction Collective 2.

⎯⎯⎯ (1993). *Critifiction: Postmodern Essays*. Albany: State University of New York Press.

⎯⎯⎯ (1982/2000). *The Twofold Vibration*. København & Los Angeles: Green Integer 45.

⎯⎯⎯ (2001). "The Necessity and Impossibility of Being a Jewish Writer." [http://www.Federman.com/rfsrcr5.htm]

Spiridon, Monica (2002). "Spaces of Memory: The City-Text" (Position paper for ACUME sub-project, "Places and Memory."
[http://www.lingue.unibo.it/acume/sb/Spiridon_Spaces_of_Memory.htm]

SESAME UNDONE

Negotiations of [Virtual] Space in Federman's blog [the laugh that laughs at the laugh...]

CAMELIA ELIAS

Y*es, I know that some people, especially the anti-logo-cen-tristes, will tell you it's the contrary, that actions are true and words false, but they're full of shit, I know what I'm talking about, and don't ask how I know, or where I got it, probably from Namredef, me I always steal things from him ...*

— Federman, *Aunt Rachel's Fur*

If asked about his long career as a writer of fiction, poetry, criticism, correspondence, journal entries, photographs and documents, and "recycled texts," Raymond Federman would probably say that the most important in his writing has been what it says about life. Ever since the early 70s when he gained recognition for his innovative works that combined fiction, criticism, and autobiography, the questions of authority and authorship, originality, meaning, appropriation, and above all, collaboration, have been on his writing agenda. Going from concerns with the textual and the literariness of a text in such works as *Surfiction* (1975) and *Critifiction* (1993), in which the question, 'what is this text about?' was clearly formulated so that it addressed itself in a metafictional gesture – the text is always about aboutness, rather than about something else – Federman's recent writing exhibits a concern with the cultural in the text, as it is mediated by personal experience, yet also through what can be theorized about the experience of others as they make an impact on the self. But here I should mention that this mediated textual aspect in any of Federman's texts has never been separated from the cultural as such, insofar as all his writings deal with the experience of the subject who, because of finding himself in a perennial state of transit, is already a cultural and textual theorist *par excellence*.

Coming to the US in the 40s as a survivor of the Holocaust, and later becoming a writer and a professor of literature, Federman has experienced what it means to write from the position of the marginal, and from there engage in strategies of embodying sites of agency through resistance. As scholars in autobiographical studies remark, here Julia Watson and Sidonie Smith following multicultural theorists such as Arjun Appadurai, "individuals as sites of agency deploy their imaginations as a social fact and a kind of work to navigate the disjunctures of global flows that create radically different self-understandings" (Smith & Watson, 2001: 44).

In terms of strategies towards self-understanding, most of Federman's writing – whether fiction or criticism – makes recourse to the figure of the double. Novels having titles such as *Double or Nothing, Take it or Leave it,* and *The Twofold Vibration* – all featuring a very engaging and engaged first person narrator – suggest that there is always a double perspective at work in the 'know thyself' project that not only activates the imagination in a dynamic and pluralistic, visual way, but also opens the space for the articulation of a radically different self-understanding. Here, I'm interested in tracing this process of self-cognition through the act of self-writing in a forum that engages several agents in a more direct way than we find in the traditional book format; namely, blogging, or writing on the internet.

With the advent of the internet the reader gains more immediate agency. Unlike in the tradition of printed matter, within which, if marginalia and scribbling are possible it is so only as a solitary act that elicits no immediate feed-back – a reader's doodling in a book is not immediately accessible to the book's author, if at all – blogging on the internet opens up for the possibility of having a dialogue between the author of the blog and the potential readers of it. Thus more than one participant, including the author, can be engaged on several levels and on texts that run on screen either in their synchronic or diachronic lay-out.

Here it is interesting to note how a writer such as Federman, who has a history, as it were, of developing the figure of the double in all his printed books – books that are also typographically challenging in this sense – manages to stretch the intrinsically playful, and also self-consciously ludic double so that it becomes a multitude of selves in the virtual space of the internet. This multitude of selves, while embodying the site of agency that is enabled by resistance to traditional modes of narration, aims at showing the fictionality of reality through virtuality. Communities are imagined, literature's ontological status is made uncertain, imagination is put in the service of displacing reality, and the life of the author is shown to be both influenced and contaminated by the lives of all those who care to respond to the author's writing with their own (ad hoc) formulations.

The idea that the self, and hence subjectivity, as always conditioned by relations is, however, not a new invention where Federman is concerned. As early as his works on Beckett in the 60s Federman has advanced the notion that all writing is self-writing, and because of that entirely fictional. This paradox – inherent in the notion that the self is never 'self' but another, to paraphrase a master cultural theorist, Arthur Rimbaud, who famously declared that "I is another" – challenges autobiography as a genre by prompting us to consider autobiography more as an act (Elizabeth Bruss), a relation (John Eakin), an attitude (George May), or a figure of reading (Paul de Man).

I argue that Federman's blog, which offers us new writings in juxtaposition with older writerly manifestations, gives us the possibility to partake in his transformations as a writer and as a person. What conditions the dynamic process between the author and his readers is the idea that all readers must also become writers if the author is to experience a sense of an emerging plural self. Quite literally, the invitation to leave a comment in the blogosphere is a constitutive act of self-representation enabled by making a direct gesture towards reducing subjectivity to the bare essentials. "I" is not only another – as it becomes the other at the moment writing takes place – but it is already Other. In cyberspace this 'already Other' is autobiographical to the extent that we can trace its anthropological virtuality through a network of links and relations.

In his book, *How our Lives become Stories* (1999), John Eakin makes the following comment in support of his claim that, if we have a sense of self to express in an autobiographical work, we do so because of our relations to others; the implicit presumption here must be that these relations are all established beyond the text, which makes autobiography already a virtual thing.

> Given the face-off between experiential accounts of the "I," on the one hand, and deconstructive analyses of the "I" as illusion on the other, my own instinct is to approach autobiography in the spirit of a cultural anthropologist, *asking what such texts can teach us about the ways in which individuals in a particular culture experience their sense of being "I"* – and in some instructive cases that prove the rule, their sense of not being an "I" (4).

What sets Federman apart, as a writer and as a cultural voice, from other writers and cultural theorists is the fact he has made the realization that in the virtual space a community of potential readers and writers is not merely imagined, but performed. Furthermore, this community is not only performed, but is itself performative. There is a move from traditional modes of narrating a life to experiencing it through the stories of others. In this sense, and in terms of agency – who says what to whom from what position – Federman aligns himself more with theorists and philosophers of the event (Badiou), performative studies (Butler), and queer studies (Halberstam) for whom agency is not only a site of resistance, but also a site for the possibility of variation. For example, for Judith Butler, subjectivity is a matter of performance that follows the rules of the game: you are what your culture says you are; if you decide to play another role, more often than not, you lose, or you pay more than that what you've bargained for. For Teresa de Laurentis, the unconscious is a site of agency: you are what your desire dictates that you are; this must mean that if desire is suppressed, your agency is limited to following others; if your desire is let loose, your agency is then channeled through desire's own excesses. Both these cases call for the regulations of the flow of negotiations which has its own set of implications for the way in which to think about disjunctures. In autobiographical studies this can be translated thus, in the words of Porter Abbot:

> [A]utobiographical narrative begins and ends in the presence of its making. To read fictively is to ask of the text: how is this complete? To read factually is to ask of the text: how is this true? To read autobiographically is to ask of the text: how does this reveal the author? (Abbot, 1988: 613)

Against this background Federman has three clearly articulated messages. 1) Have some fun! Nobody is perfect; 2) Instruct! But acknowledge the limit of your knowledge; 3) Subvert politics! Mess up the authorial voice: 'who speaks what to whom, on what and whose authority' must be regarded within the frame of the personal, which is seen both as a risk and as an opportunity. Thus the mode of expression in the blog is set up. Here, the fact that the line from Beckett's *Watt*, [the laugh that laughs at the laugh] that plays on the question of 'what' (is this all about), is framed by square brackets is not incidental either. What Federman shows is that the question, 'what is this text about?' is an impossible question that can only be addressed through role-playing. Role-playing is a form of scriptedness that invites us to consider the function of simultaneity and plurality in the juxtaposition of texts and voices, writers and readers. What is at stake is the question of the extent to which each party is willing to open up a space for the others to occupy, and by occupying, to read. In this sense, the question, 'what is this text about?' becomes a question of space, one that draws the writer to writing for what occasions the reader's response. The aim is to have the reader read for the event of writing, rather than read for the instruction, inspiration, or enchantment.

Writing Selves on Paper

In order to better understand what is at stake in Federman's blog, I offer here a brief excursion into one of Federman's most exciting books, *The Twofold Vibration* (1982), in which the emergence of the writer's self is mediated through negotiations of variations on the first person narrative. The short discussion of *The Twofold Vibration* will serve to illustrate how the tension between (distant) history, as formulated on paper, and (immediate) history, as formulated through anticipating media interventions, diminishes. In this work *par excellence* Federman explores the extent to which one can recount one's personal past and history through the deployment of pseudo-selves whose function is to undo history through engaging in a discourse that can be termed *immemorable*. This is to say that past events are not remembered in any representational way, but are preformed beyond memory and beyond the memorial.

In a gesture that aims at performativity Federman thus declares in *The Twofold Vibration* that "History is bankrupt" (1982: 234). This suggests that history, like money, is a liability in the hands of investors who can lose it, gain it again, invest in it, sell it, buy it, conceal it, reveal it, make it available. All these fluctuating and conflicting aspects of history are in fact recurrent in all of his fictional works and point to a world of potentiality. As a subject in a historical context, one relates to history's potential by exhibiting what Federman calls a "sense of historical possibilities" (254).

On a general level, Federman's works are saturated with making history, and particularly personal history, an active part of memory, which never settles with 'solid,' or 'simple,' facts, but rather develops possibilities and potentialities around factual certainties. "I am often asked," Federman writes, "as a survivor of the Holocaust and as a writer: 'Federman tell us the story of your survival.' And I can only answer: 'There is no story. My life is the story. Or rather, the story is my life'" (Federman, 2001).

All Federman's fictional work is concerned with construing variations on statements such as these, which mark a demand for distinguishing history from story, reality from fiction, and space from time. Federman's capacity to think historically is enforced in the idea of remembrance as a narrative strategy: one writes in order to remember and one remembers in order to be able to reveal. "It is necessary to speak," he furthermore says,

> [T]o write, and keep on speaking and writing (lest we forget) about the Jewish Holocaust during the Nazi period even if words cannot express this monstrous event. It is impossible to speak or write about the Holocaust because words cannot express this monstrous event (2001).

For Federman, therefore, history is a dialectical bind that involves the transmission of that which is both necessary and impossible.

His notion of history is not defined by a rejection of it as an ideology, but by creating a mode of discourse in which history is open to possibilities. This openness is also what mediates between the real and the fictional grounding of both the telling of a story in life and life in the telling of a story. The example that best illustrates what it means to approach history "from a potential point of view," as Federman puts it in *The Twofold Vibration*, is a passage from his essay "The Necessity and Impossibility of Being a Jewish Writer." Here Federman actually quotes himself from his novel *Take It or Leave It* (1976), which suggests that the negotiation for a space in which the character can develop vacillates between making choices for a genre and just settling for whatever it is: fiction, autobiography, or hybrids across, such as *autofiction*, or *autobiofiction*. The protagonist, a French Jew survivor of the Holocaust says the following:

> Take my case for instance. What do you think I would be today if it were not for Hitler? Do you know what I would be today? I mean if nothing had happened. No war, no occupation, no collaboration, no deportation, no extermination – no Holocaust. Yes, do you know what I would be today? A tailor. A little Jewish tailor slaving in a tailor shop on Boulevard des Italiens in Paris. Or else an instituteur in some intellectually retarded school in the province of France. But let me assure you [and here the protagonist and the author merge into one], I would not be a writer (an experimental writer, I am told), dealing with such an important topic as the Holocaust. No, I would not be here, making up my life as I go along. Certainly not. Therefore, funny as it may seem, disturbing and grotesque as it may sound, Hitler in a

way was my savior. Yes, I know it's laughable, preposterous, but it's true (2001).

What this passage suggests is that fiction validates an element of potential truth, or reality in history. And what Federman is trying to say is that history would not be history if it were not open to both possibility and potential. Possibility and potential create excessiveness in relation to the theme of survival. Survival is rendered possible, insofar as it is either based or conditioned on a memory or 'unconcealment' of what has the potential to pass into oblivion. But while survival itself cannot be expressed by memory, it is nevertheless a manifestation of memory. As he further elaborates in *The Twofold Vibration*:

[T]he fact of being a survivor, of living with one's death behind, in a way makes you free, free and irresponsible toward your own end, of course you feel a little guilty while you're surviving because there is this thing about your past, your dead past and all that, but you have to get on with things, sustain your excessiveness (Federman, 1982: 99–100).

Survival as excessiveness, for Federman, is the same as writing disengaged from history, and yet also a manifestation of historical events unfolding in a narrative that engages several voices at the first person level.

But here, Federman's relation to history goes beyond a mere re-creative project of contemporary innovative fiction, a project which, as Marcel Cornis-Pope notes, has been at the heart of postmodern writing in its challenge of the great "metarecits" – Cornis-Pope, however, is here more interested in whether it is true or even necessary for postmodern fiction to move beyond history (Cornis-Pop, 1994: 1). Narratives such as Federman's engage with affirmations of and beliefs in the "end of history," as Vattimo and Lyotard posited, but unlike both Vattimo and Lyotard, Federman offers a different perspective. He puts an end to the 'end of history' story, not by going beyond, but rather behind history, by backing it up from a position of potentiality and possibility. What I'm saying is that history never happens other than a story whose event is potentiality itself, on the one hand, and the possibility to repeat itself, on the other hand. This position assumes virtual proportions in Federman's later works, but I will elaborate on this a little further on.

What remains general, however, is that story telling, for Federman, is developed as a "tradition of the immemorial," to use Giorgio Agamben's term, as it follows a line of questioning what validates writing under the sign of history. Federman's own questions are based on the assumption that history itself is not history, but language and tradition without which a "sense of historical possibilities" would not be possible. Here I would like to introduce a variation on Federman's constant attempt to either explain or bridge the gap between necessity and impossibility, by proposing that his narratives are driven forward by an element of the immemorial, namely that which occupies a space simultaneously in the active telling of the events which are posited as un-narratable, and in the static representation of the events as potential points of view. In other words, Federman's narratives carry within them a concrete manifestation of memory which they want to transmit, and they carry as well the vehicle for transmission, that is, transmissibility itself which is conceived ontologically as unthematized in any memorial form. For example, what interests Federman in his fiction is not to make central the extermination of the Jews, but rather participate instead in "the erasure of that extermination" (Federman, 2001). He needs, however, to transmit the memory of that event in order to be able to erase its ontological manifestation in the form of extermination: steal back the voices of those who have lost the potential to narrate their own stories in the face of their selves having been deleted from history.

Federman's concept of history, in this sense, as a mediation between a story and its audience finds resonance in Agamben's statement at the beginning of his essay "Tradition of the Immemorial":

> Every reflection on tradition must begin with the assertion that before transmitting anything else, human beings must first of all transmit language to themselves [....] What has already been transmitted in every tradition, the *architraditum* and the *primum* of every tradition, is the thing of thinking (Agamben, 1999: 104).

Thus we come to the core of the matter: if language and tradition give us a sense of historical possibilities, then the thinking – the already transmitted thinking, must also be thinking about transmissibility, about what remains unthematized in the mediation between a story and us, ourselves in context and our potential, "I," "me," and "we," or in other words, the first person. Here I would like to argue that storytelling, for Raymond Federman, is an act of provocation which engages the reader in a refashioning of history by constructing a narrative that transforms memory, time, and place into potentials for a *topos* where the act of narrating in the first person plural becomes the memory of history.

No longer believing in the power of fiction which makes recourse to the autobiographical genre that relies on the use of memory for the narrated events, Federman claims that personal memory is superseded by imagination, insofar as a writer is capable of transforming the elements of his life as part of history into a story. Here Federman contrasts differing views on modernist auto-biographical writing with postmodern fiction. As he writes:

> Until very recently one read novels – especially those written in the first person – as though they were mere autobiographies, and it was assumed that the writer merely wrote what he **remembered** of his life, of his youth, of his family, of his amorous adventures. Consequently, **memory** (voluntarily or involuntarily) was considered the sole mechanism that made personal or autobiographical fiction possible […] Contemporary experimental fiction is no longer written as **remembered events**, but on the basis of **invented events** which seem to be happening (very much as in the cinema right before the reader's eyes, in the present (Federman, 1993: 100–102) (author's emphasis).

Federman's distinction between remembered and invented events is mediated by the trajectory that imagination takes in the act of transmitting. In this context, history is thus the memory of the immemorial, as it were, or the memory of the present past. Giving himself as an example of the avant-garde writer who construes a narrative in the future in order to say something about the past, Federman deals with a present which always presents itself in a hypothetical form. One of the points that he makes in his narratives of survival is that, if he had died in the concentration camps, he would still have been able to write and tell about his death. His present situation as a survivor enables him to imagine himself dead, alive, or somewhere in between, which is to say both, dead and alive. The memory of that kind of surviving, then, is transformed into a present from which concrete elements that shape history are absent, or await actualization.

Federman's strategy of narration by going behind history is an investigation into the immemorial, implicit in the transmissibility of the history of the Holocaust, which is posited always as an unfinished story throughout all of his work. As he recounts in almost all of his narratives, whether fictional or otherwise, the Nazis had an unfinished business with him. As a child of twelve in 1942, when the Nazis were out on a mission of rounding up and collecting Jews in Paris, Federman was pushed by his mother into a closet where he remained for two days. Following his escape, he was nevertheless caught at the train station and put on a train to the concentration camps. He escaped from that train, but as he tells us in *The Twofold Vibration* via an embedded first person narrator, he escaped not because he ever intended to escape, but because of an instinct. Hunger made him seize the opportunity to jump on a parallel train while his own train was making a stop. There were potatoes to be had. Potentiality's own twofold vibration in Federman's intent, on the one hand to escape his hunger, and on the other, to follow the fate of his father, mother, and two sisters who all died, remains for Federman a question of hypothetical history caught between unfinished and unthematized time. The fate of his family, which he would have shared, or he thinks he ought to have shared, finds vibration in the excessiveness of survival.

Implicit in Federman's dilemma, then, is the thematization of an act which never took place – let's call it the act of dying, dying in the past – but which constitutes, however, Federman's life. Insofar as his life is based on a perpetual potential for dying in the past, Federman's discourse thus remains in a state similar to a transmission devoid of transmissibility. And this is the crux of Federman's narrative voice: how to express the necessity and impossibility of individual experience, when it is based on collective memory and a discourse that is not one's own. Agamben says:

> Implicit in every act of transmission, it [transmissibility] must remain unfinished, and at the same time, unthematized. The tradition of transmissibility is therefore immemorially contained in every specific tradition, and this immemorial legacy, this transmission of unconcealment, constitutes human language as such (Agamben, 1999: 105).

Against the background of the unfinished business of dying when everyone else you cherished did, Federman's works must be seen as an exchange between memory, or unconcealment, and oblivion or concealment, past and present, story and history all mediated by the immemorial legacy inherent in transmissibility. Memory which combats erasure functions as a vehicle for the representation of what is under erasure, the "X." For Federman, the four Xes, which he always writes in lieu of the representation of the exterminated family, represent a metonymic code that cracks the metaphor of concealment. When we are told that the Xes, that is, the family, have been turned into lampshades we begin to understand Federman's "sense of historical possibilities," as lampshades indeed have the potential to be the vehicle for illumination. The tradition of this kind of illumination is, however, bound to remain unfinished and unthematized, and hence immemorial. In this sense Federman's Xes have the potential to shed light on the kind of writing that keeps history in mind.

For Federman, writing which makes recourse to personal history spanning a series of dramatic events (World War II, the Holocaust, exile, immigration to America) is a means of connecting what Monika Fludernik calls "the subversive potential" (in Cornis-Pop) of the second person narrator to what I would call the "immemorial potential" of the first person plural narrator. The interplay between first, second, and third person narrators, culminating in the collective narrator/narratee of the first person plural further indicates that the reader's referential field itself becomes a potential for situating history not in context, but in memory.

The way Federman deals with the demand for writing which relies on impossible words is by creating a world of narrators who are all schmucks in all 300 or so Jewish senses of the word. These narrators create a situation of 'shmuckiness' for the writer, usually a narrator and a protagonist at the same time. This 'shmuckiness' of the situation is always shown by the narrator to interfere with the transmission of the narrative that the protagonist is invested in delivering. For instance, *The Twofold Vibration,* a narrative about an old man awaiting to be deported to the colonies, not on earth but in space, begins with a consideration of its own agency and point of view, namely "a potential point of view, premembering the future rather than remembering the past" (Federman, 1982: 10). For Federman, the potential point of view is initially represented by a third person singular pronoun. This pronoun, while always embodying the potential to become the first person singular, ultimately develops into the first person plural as this example illustrates:

> [T]he old man was born in 1918, like my father, coincidentally, or for that matter like me, fictitiously speaking, what's the difference, we are all extensions of one another, the living as well as the dead, we all overlap within the twofold vibration of history (11).

Later in the book it is disclosed that "he," "I," and "we" are second-hand tellers, addressers and addressees of the second person singular and plural, "you."

The old man's story is recounted to a narrator named "Federman" by his two friends Moinous and Namredef, who tell the story of the old man in the first person plural, interchanging with a narrative voice of both the old man as well as that of "Federman" in the first person singular. A fifth voice is added to the Babylon – that of the author who both participates directly in the events at all levels, and makes meta-comments on all levels. Moinous, a composite French name based on the pronouns *moi* (me) and *nous* (we, us), and Namredef, Federman spelled backwards, are two indirect protagonists. When they learn that the old man, who is nameless, is about to be shipped to the space colonies, they attempt to stop the deportation for which no reasons are given. Their investigation into the unknown reasons takes place mainly in bars and restaurants of first class food and comfort where they occasionally meet "Federman" the narrator, who has commissioned a full report from them.

The narrative structure is divided between active protagonists (the old man and Federman) and passive protagonists (Moinous and Namredef). Technically, the old man and Federman are "extradiegetic" and "homodiegetic" narrators (Genette, 1972: 256). Their narrative, which they narrate themselves, is, however, mediated by Moinous and Namredef, who are "intradiegetic" and "hetero/homodiegetic" narrators. Moinuous and Namredef act as fictional narrators insofar as they are the creation of Federman the narrator who placed them in the story for the purpose of creating dynamism and a sense of chronology.

The story features a struggle for the primacy over voice and the desire to invert the active and passive roles. Moinous and Namredef often complain about their "plotless existence and its lack of dramatic development" (Federman, 1982: 232), and in spite of their taking pride in their attributes as characters, they remain unsatisfied with their fictional status. For instance, Moinous is very keen on details and always gives elaborate descriptions of objects and colours, however irrelevant, while Namredef sees himself as a character of insight. He often interrupts Moinous by offering short comments on the narrated event. But while they are both good at reporting, they are very bad at interpreting and cannot decipher symbols. As they recount the old man's travelling through Europe, where he is either visiting concentration camps or casinos, Moinous and Namredef do not realize that they themselves make up the link between such incongruent events. Whenever there is a jump from one extreme to another, the time between the events is Moinous and Namredef's time, when they become active participants in the narrative. When they all go to see Wagner's *Parsifal* immediately following the old man's visiting the concentration camp in Dachau, they engage in a discourse of disapproval, taking on the cliché of the burden of the suffering Jew. Objecting to their complaint, the old man's voice merges with that of the author who often criticizes the approach to art taken by many Jewish writers who feel the need to respond to what they think is demanded of them, namely to assume responsibility for the entire history and suffering of the Jewish people. "Everything in art is contradictory," the old man says in a tone of exasperation following the Wagner performance. Irritated by the crowd sharing his enthusiasm, he urges Moinous and Namredef to get out of the streets. The theme of contradiction then establishes the relation between extra/intra/hypodiegetic narrative levels and suddenly 5 voices intercalate, as the following passage illustrates:

Let's get the fuck out of here, the old man suddenly said as he rushed us into the street

I don't understand why you get so worked up, Namredef told his old friend, I really don't get it, after all you are the one who wanted to come here, who drove forty-eight hours like a maniac to get us here, the old man was walking in long strides, almost running, Namredef and Moinous trotting along to keep up with him, they are both short and a bit flabby, Is it because you're Jewish, asked Namredef totally out of breath, I'm Jewish too and I don't get excited like you when I am in the midst of Germans, you can't blame them all, is it because your entire family was exterminated by the Nazis, so what, mine too was remade into lampshades at Auschwitz, or have you forgotten

And mine too, mine too, intervened Moinous who was holding on to his side as he trotted along splashing in the rain

The old man shrugged his shoulders, It has nothing to do with that, and besides I'm not worked up, I'm just being philosophical, that's all, the two of you always confuse ideology with sentiment, yes it's amazing how you two schnorrers always have to reduce everything to your Jewish sentimentality

oh you people didn't know Namredef and Moinous are Jewish too, well I haven't mentioned it because I thought it was obvious, and anyway this is not their story, they are incidental here, they have been introduced simply for the convenience of the narrative, to help along, to allow some shifts of point of view and some creative free play (153-154).

There is an ideological point in the use of the first person plural here that Federman's narrators illustrate in their first person singular narrative which always relates to a second person, "you", a narrative voice that becomes personified as "us." If "the second person is *par excellence* the sign of a relation" as Brian MacHale puts it, the first person plural can be said to designate an immemorial potential. The schmuck, or here, *schnorrer,* is a figure of immemorial narration, insofar as its character establishes itself as an authoritative non-voice charged with strong motivations for the articulation of history. The schmuck in the first person plural is not confrontational, but negotiating. What he negotiates are acts of transmission, acts of remembrance, story and history, and acts which rely on words, both possible and impossible words. These acts are all employed as vehicles for the demand of necessity. The first person plural is implied as a key moment in reference to the immemorial, which indicates that the immemorial is now a concrete potential of a historical possibility. As far as I can gather, for Federman the demand of necessity can only be expressed in a convoluted, black ink form. As he asserts:

It's all there, you schmucks, inside the words, teller and told, survivors and victims unified into a single design, if you read the text carefully then you'll see appear before you on the shattered white space the people drawn by the black words, flattened and disseminated on the surface of the paper inside the black ink-blood, that was the challenge, never to speak the reality of the event but to render it concrete into the blackness of the words (225).

Federman's first person plural drawn against the background of the "you," of the "you schmucks," and forced into participating in the narrative is a means of disclosing the 'plot' against traditional modes of narration. The reader's expectation has been set up and one realizes that one has been framed as one of the schmucks referred to in the text. But there is always a problem with schmucks, one that involves reading. While the unspeakable event that Federman calls upon can, indeed, be rendered concrete in the words, what if nobody reads? And if someone does read, how well will they be able to do it? It takes a particular Devil to read not only what is unspeakable, but to read the unspeakable itself. Yet, having a sense of historical possibility means being able to run the risk of being a schmuck, championing a position between impossibility and necessity. By assigning agency to writing itself, or to the event of writing, Federman expands the reader's referential field to include the potential for situating history not in context, but in memory as the vehicle for the transmissibility of writing. The concreteness of words is not merely a manifestation of potential reading, but a manifestation of reading carefully and attentively. The schmuck does not speak any reality; he transmits it.

Reading Selves on Screen

If we return to Federman's blogosphere, we can make the assumption that the figure of the schmuck *par excellence* opens up the notion that especially in virtual space, nothing is protected from reading. Thus the demand to distinguish between Federman's own voice and the voice of his readers who write comments, or to distinguish the 'telling' function from the 'showing' function of the uploaded texts, is here exceeded by the very virtuality of the cyberspace which creates the writer in its own image, namely that of unreality. Yet again Federman brings himself in that impossible and abstract situation – one that he borrows from Beckett: "I can't go on, I'll go on" – which refers to his survival. If writing is possible at all, as he so many times repeatedly reminds us in all of his works, it is so because it is also impossible. One writes not with a sense of finality, or because one can't help oneself, but with a sense of openness, because one wants to learn from others. One writes because one survives through others whom one can write about. At least this is one of the messages that the blog puts forth. The vehicle for this message is language as a game. What one does in the blogosphere is permute with and transmute questions such as 'who's who?' 'what's what?' and 'where's where?' into and across various, different, and radically different cultural manifestations. Seen in this light, these questions become the key to the 'Open Sesame' of subjectivity.

While Federman is adamant in urging us to keep writing and speaking (in his printed works and now even more so in cyberspace), the very transmission of the words, which are impossible to write and utter, remains a fundamental problem without obvious solutions. If we were to employ the well-known magical metaphor for the kind of search that links writing with an imperative or a demand, 'Open Sesame,' we would realize that this cry assumes a different manifestation in Federman, insofar as he believes that writing is an impossible task. Stealing is more like it, and just as Ali Baba managed to retrieve some of the fortune that the 40 Arabian thieves had hidden in their magical cave that would only open by shouting the secret code, Federman makes a similar gesture: steal from the many and undo the myth of continuity.

In Hindu legends the sesame seed represents a symbol of immortality. If visualized graphically in the context of the story from the Arabian Nights collection, an opening of immortality would necessarily involve the creation of a major gap. If we keep this image in mind, we can say that continuity is only possible, if it gets to be discontinued first. In Federman's *oeuvre* the demand to 'open writing' and then 'close writing' constitutes a gesture towards bridging the gap between necessity and impossibility. Only, this gesture is mediated by a moment in which words are stolen. Thus the sesame is undone.

Federman's turning to the world of virtual texts has the potential to answer the question regarding the consequences and implications of nobody reading anything anymore, especially books. In an interview with Larry McCaffrey in 1980, he talks about the notion of "opening up a space" in which to write fiction. As I have suggested so far, for Federman, the dynamics in the act of opening up writing through stealing imagined words contributes to the creation of a fiction that is also entirely preoccupied with projections of the self in the future. The fictional self which emerges as a future potential is bound to re-inscribe tradition and the sense of a collective fate expressed as a universal belief à la 'everybody died in Auschwitz' within a framework of virtual experience: in cyberspace nobody is dead because nobody is alive either. In [the laugh that laughs at the laugh] it is clear that one way of also dealing with the perception that the Jew is part of a single unified group is by emphasizing the ultimate collectivity and connectivity that the Internet as a space accommodating more than 40 thieves confers to the individual. The point in Federman is that the minute we leave a message (as a comment on one of his posts) is also the minute we become part of his own Jewishness, as we write ourselves over to that specific experience too. It is this minute that lends us an extra function in our reading capacity. This function revolves around the readers' possibility to 'graph' the author's 'auto' perception in their own pseudo-biographical gesture that they extends.

If we keep the 'stealing' metaphor in mind, we realize that cyberspace is the space *par excellence* for exchanging identities, pseudo or otherwise, precisely through appropriation. As mentioned already, in Federman's blog, we find an array of texts posted for this medium alone, but we also find older texts that he recycles, re-appropriates and reprises, either for commercial purposes, or for the sake of simply emphasizing the fact that if writing and living are connected, as he otherwise insists they are in all of his works, then this connection is necessarily given through and mediated by fragments.

What we can observe from the outset is that the texts written for the blog, in some way or another, not only reflect, but also complement older texts. One of the posts, for instance, on "Statues of Kings," can be said to not only complement the post based on a quotation from "About Writers and Writing" (1996), but also mirror its nerve. Let's have a look.

Statues of Kings

Statues of kings can be categorized as follows:

1. Kings seated on:

a) a throne
b) a stool
c) a boulder
d) a horse (often)
e) a donkey (rarely)
f) a quadruped (an elephant or a camel in exotic places)
g) the shoulders of another man (occasionally)
h) the roof of a building (extremely rare occasions)

2. Kings standing on:

a) the ground
b) a podium
c) a stage (official occasions)
d) a stool with a back
e) a stool without a back
f) a pedestal (often)
g) a horse or any other animal (awkwardly)
h) a man lying on the ground (unusual circumstances)

3. Kings seated or standing with:

a) their arms falling to their sides
b) the left or right hand on the chest
c) both hands on the chest

d) one hand in the pocket of their trousers
e) both hands in the pockets of their trousers
f) one hand on top of their head (almost never)
g) their legs crossed (very often)
h) their eyes closed (only when they are dead)

4. Kings lying down:

a) usually during insurrections or revolutions
b) normally while making love
c) when they are dead

About writers and writing

1. The overbearing arrogance of writers is true, just ask us.
2. If one sits on one's ass all day, in due course one will enlarge one's asshole. This is why writers are classified as Big Assholes.
3. When the writer announces that he or she has found his or her voice, you may interpret that to mean:
   a) _____
   b) _____
   c) _____
   d) _____
   None of the above _____.

4. Writing is a lot like fucking, but only like it, not it.

5. I never met a writer I liked, says the writer into the mirror.

6. Writing is not [we insist] the living repetition of life. Moreover, all writing is done [in our opinion] hapharzardly.

7. Writing is such a burden, especially because of its manual aspect (Federman, 1996).

In cyberspace, when one says: "Open Sesame" the treasures found inside will consist of a privilege: to have the last word, which has the potential to undo any final authority, final authorship, and final authorization.

Federman understands this, and so do I. We thus bond in the cuts and (w)holes of our Jewishness. The last word, now, belongs to me, yet it is graphed as a stolen mark; the mark of the "I" as myself, but also the mark of the "eye" that sees me as another. I'm stealing Rimbaud's line and pass it on to Federman: "Je est un autre." In this vein, this is what I wrote to Federman not so long ago, in connection with another discourse on his writing and delivered as a talk at a university in Romania.

> Ray, your post reminds me of one of my favorite writers of aphorisms, whom you undoubtedly know: Stainslaw Jerzy Lec. He said once: "even on the throne, the pants wear out". The image of kings in whatever position, lying down, sitting, or running around merely displaying their garments with occasional holes in them, makes me laugh. It occurs to me that this post complements very nicely your other post, in which you quote yourself, "About Writers and Writing." Perhaps you are suggesting that the question for writers still remains similar to that which Alice in

Wonderland poses: who is to be master? Who is to be king of writing? Any thoughts? I'm writing as we speak (or write) a paper for an invited presentation at Babes-Bolyai University in Cluj, dealing, of course, with you as a master. Words are sexy, you said to me not long ago, so now I want to ask, even if it's slightly unrelated: have you ever been caught with your 'writerly' pants down? And if so, what was it like to be seen (or read) in the nakedness of the image? (I'm curious about the signs of circumcision; cuts and holes can be interesting to read).

As ever, Camelia Elias

And as the story goes, not only did Federman reply to my query in a private mail that fills 10 pages (an edited version of this constitutes the epilogue to this volume), but he also posted a conversation with one of the Romanian students present at my talk (see "A Conversation with Miloi"). And then some of my own students wanted to post something in connection with a class I was teaching at the time on autobiography.

The moral of this story? If Beckett's line confuses us: "I can't go on, I'll go on," we can turn to reading. Thus reading must go on. Though stop reading this. Read some blogs instead.

References

Abbot, Porter (1988). "Autobiography, Autography, Fiction: Groundwork for a Taxonomy of Textual Categories." *New Literary History*, 19.

Agamben, Giorgio (1999). *Potentialities: Collected Essays in Philosophy*. Trans. Daniel Heller-Roazen. Stanford: Stanford University Press.

Appadurai, Arjun (1994). "Disjuncture and Difference in the Global Cultural Economy." *Colonial Discourse and Post-Colonial Theory: A Reader*. Ed. Patrick Williams and Laura Chrisman. New York: Columbia University Press.

Badiou, Alain (2005). *Being and Event*. Trans. Oliver Feltham. New York: Continuum.

Bruss, Elizabeth (1976). *Autobiographical Acts. The Changing Situation of a Literay Genre*. Baltimore and London: The Johns Hopkins University Press.

Butler, Judith (1990). *Gender Trouble: Feminism and the Subversion of Identity*. Chapman & Hall: Routlege.

Cornis-Pope, Marcel (1994). "From Cultural Provocation to Narrative Cooperation: Innovative Uses of the Second Person in Raymond Federman's Fiction". *Style*. Dekalb, Vol. 28, Issue 3.

De Laurentis, Teresa (1990). "Eccentric Subjects: Feminist Theory and Historical Consciousness." *Feminist Studies* 16, no. 1.

De Man, Paul (1979) "Autobiography as De-facement." *Modern Language Notes 94*.

Eakin, John (1999) *How our Lives Become Stories*. Ithaca, New York: Cornell U Press.

Federman, Raymond (1971/1991). *Double or Nothing: A Real Fictitious Discourse*. Fiction Collective 2.

_____ (1976/1997). *Take It or Leave It*. FC2, Illinois.

_____ (1993). *Critifiction: Postmodern Essays*. Albany: State University of New York Press.

_____ (1982/2000). *The Twofold Vibration*. København & Los Angeles: Green Integer 45.

_____ (2001). "The Necessity and Impossibility of Being a Jewish Writer". [http://www.Federman.com/rfsrcr5.htm]

_____ FEDERMAN'S BLOG [the laugh that laughs at the laugh...] [http://raymondfederman.blogspot.com/]

"Statues of Kings"
[http://raymondfederman.blogspot.com/search?q=statues]

"Fragments og Writing: About Writers and Writing"
[http://www.federman.com/rffict5.htm]

"A Conversation with Miloi"
[http://raymondfederman.blogspot.com/search?q=miloi]

Genette, Gerard (1972). *Figures III*. (Vol. 1-3 Collection Tel Ques). Paris: Editions du Seuil.

McCaffery, Larry and Federman, Raymond (1983) "An Interview with Raymond Federman." *Contemporary Literature*, Vol. 24, No. 3, Autumn.

May, George (1979). "Autobiography in the Eighteenth Century." *The Author in His Work: Essays on a Problem in Criticism*. Ed. Louis L. Mortz & Aubrey Williams New Haven: Yale University Press.

Smith, Sidonie and Watson, Julia (2001). *Reading Autobiography: A Guide for Interpreting Life Narratives*. Minneapolis: University of Minnesota Press.

EPILOG[ICAL] ENCOUNTERS

CAMELIA ELIAS & RAYMOND FEDERMAN

If it ever becomes necessary for you to eat a book, out of despair or out of some primal need, then eat the telephone book, for it is the only book in your library which came free. Except, of course, the books you stole.

– Federman, *Eating Books*

Bent Vibrations

In the year 1989 I came to Denmark as a refugee from Romania. Talking to the immigration police at the impressive Kastrup airport in Copenhagen, I could tell that the women who gave me the preliminary search – as custom is when one declares oneself a fugitive – were baffled at my parcel. All I had with me were a couple of books, fairytales and novels, and a couple of *haute couture* dresses. Odd combination, they thought. Odd combination for a refugee, they furthermore thought. One of the books was a volume that comprised two works in one. These works were Raymond Federman's *The Twofold Vibration* (translated into Romanian as *Indoita Vibratie*) and *Smiles in Washington Square* (*Zîmbete în Washington Square*).

I didn't think much at the time about the Romanian translation of *The Twofold Vibration*, as 'Bent Vibrations.' I took it at face value, and considered it a straightforward title. My English was rudimentary at the time. Since then I've learned to appreciate the many facets and layers that such a word as 'twofold' has. Now I particularly prefer the connotation 'twice as great.' In my scholarly papers on Federman, since my first naïve encounter with his works, 'twice as great' has been the operative phrase on all levels: descriptive, analytical, and evaluative. If Federman proved anything in his long writing career, then one could say that he has proved to be twice as good as any other writer. At this point I could venture into another full-fledged paper on Federman, and explain some more, twofold, threefold, and manifold. But the present volume should suffice. In itself it is already twofold as it dares to entangle a meta-discursive language with a more personal take on Federman. Nothing else would cut it.

Already in Karlstad, when we presented work on Federman, we have discovered that writing on Federman is a special affair. The four of us were very enthusiastic, albeit disappointed to realize that there were very few people who knew about Federman. Hence we took it upon ourselves to preach to the unenlightened. As it goes with prophets, however, such projects can only go two ways in terms of people's responses: the converted may say, "yes," the skeptics may be more dismissive: "there go the nerds."

As this volume has been written against two background demands: 'keep on preaching!' and "celebrate Federman at 80!" one more point should be stressed before we render here an actual encounter with Federman, not beyond texts, but certainly beyond textuality. We have suggested that what makes Federman such a good writer is the fact that he has an acute sense of style. This style, however, does not stem from a mere consideration of highly aesthetic philosophies, but from careful consideration of readers. In Federman's conviction, all readers are ideal readers. Within this context, I see it befit in my capacity as an editor to end on a note that offers the readers of this volume an insight into what a great master can do: teach how to read. Within Federman's own contexts for reading, his stories become our histories, his status our cult, and his memory our selves.

As with Federman, then, we take reading and writing about reading to levels where language is inflected, bent, turned on and against itself, bitten and eaten by its tail. This reading tale is what allows us ultimately to both ask and answer the question: "Am I an autobiographical writer? Yes and No." We let Federman vibrate.

Dear Camelia[1]

I read your essay and – yes – it's a *superbe* new approach to my writing – especially your reading of TTV – not just what is says about the sordid past – but about how it is said with those multiple voices while reading I was scribbling in the margins of your essay –

---

[1] This is a slightly edited version of an email sent to me by Federman on December 1, 2007, in response to a draft for an invited presentation at Babes-Bolyai University in Cluj on Dec. 3, 2007. The permission to reprint Federman's private text has been given to me by Federman himself with these words: "you have my permission to use and abuse whatever you need and want from my work including my body." This is what I call a generous author, *in extremis*. I thanked Raymond for both his words and for his body.

here are some thoughts —

on the first page I lifted (notice I didn't say steal but I should have) this sentence —

"one writes in order to remember, and one remembers in order to be able to reveal"[2] [70]

and I wrote it in the big book that seats on my desk with the title:

Federman's aphorisms / Les aphorismes de Federman —

maybe some day after I have changed tense somebody will find this book and write a doctoral dissertation claiming that Federman was a prophet or a philosopher or simply a madman — there is madness in that book — and a lot of thievery —

anyway —

I always laugh when I reread that passage from TIOLI where Frenchy claims that Hitler was his savior —

but rereading that passage in the context of your *essai* it becomes a kind of manifesto for Federman's writing — projecting himself backward in order to better project himself forward — from the little Jewish tailor [most of Federman's uncles were tailors] he could have been to the preposterous experimental writer and madman he became —

you are right to insist on the potential truth —

I don't think I invented it — but I think I make good use of it —

I have often said that my death is behind me and that's why I feel so free to do whatever I do write sleep eat smoke pot make love masturbate write read sleep play golf travel and son on —

---

[2] Federman's references here can be found in my essay, 'Sesame Undone,' in this volume. Where he quotes me directly, I indicate the page numbers here in square brackets. The pages that Federman refers to are the pages of the text I sent him in 2007.

I am reacting here to that quotation in your text on page 3 from TTV which makes you state that survival as excessiveness is the same as writing disengaged from history ....
It is true that I do everything excessively and often irresponsibly – but never with guilt
digression – the French version of *My Body in Nine Parts* [have you read that book?] – *Mon Corps en Neuf Parties* has been staged in France by two different theater companies, and is having lots of success, at least according to the two articles I just got – this will interest you – especially in terms of how my work is finding new places new spaced to corrupt their minds and bodies – I'll attach the two articles –
I like what you say on page 4 and elsewhere – about bridging the gap – which in my fiction is often referred to as the precipice –
digression – have I ever sent you the play I wrote called *The Precipice?* – it might interest you –

x x x x

I hope, Camelia, I am not boring you with all these digressions and reflections –
your *essai* really excited me intellectually –
digressive question – why you are so smart and write so well? – so well in English too –
Page 5. I made all kinds of little xxxxx in the margin next to this paragraph – little xxxx is the way I express agreement and admiration when I read something that moves me or makes me think –
I quote the whole sentence which caused me to shake my head in agreement and admiration:

"I would like to argue that storytelling for Federman is an act of provocation which engages the reader in a refashioning of history by constructing a narrative that transforms memory, time, and place into potentials for a *topos* where the act of narrating in the first person plural becomes the memory of history." [74]

Absolutely brilliant Camelia. This sentence summarizes everything I write and how I write it. To put it in a more intellectual fashion – you have articulated here my theory of narrative – and I didn't even know I was doing it this way –

Page 6. This sentence –

"One of the points that he makes in his narratives of survival is that, if he had died in the concentration camps, he would still have been able to write and tell about his death." [75]

Yes I would have premembered it from – as my old master once put it – from the reverse of farness –

this is why I often say – my death is behind me – it's true – I can even remember it –

which sometimes leads me to make this preposterous statement – I am immortal until proven otherwise –

I scribbled all over page 7 [75-76].

Lots of little xxxxxxx after this sentence –

"The fate of his family, which he would have shared, or he thinks he ought to have shared, finds vibration in the excessiveness of survival" [76] –

ah yes excessiveness –

in the novel I just finished – in French – which I hope you will soon read – it's called *Chut: Histoire d'une Enfance* – yes I have finally managed to write about the 13 years that preceded the closet – in a way I have just written the end of the big book I've been writing for

more than 40 years – my end is in my beginning – as Eliot put it – for me, my beginning is in my end –
in that novel I describe a scene in which little Raymond is playing doctor with his little sister Jacqueline –
a voice comes into the text to ask if I was imposing on my sister when I was examining her scientifically – here is my answer to that question –

x x x x

Federman, rien n'est normal avec toi. Peut-être que ta soeur n'aimait pas ce que tu lui faisais. Peut-être qu'elle pansied que tu t'impasse.

Je sais pas ce que ma petite soeur pansied ou ressentait. Mais elle riait. Peut-être qu'elle ressentait ce que W. B. Yeats a si bien exprimé dans son beau poème Leda and the Swan. The Shudder in the loins.

Mes soeurs n'ont jamais connu le frisson au bas du ventre. Cela leur a été refusé. Peut-être est-ce la raison pour laquelle j'ai tant abusé de ce frisson, pour compenser le plaisir et la douceur Que mes soeurs n'ont jamais connus.

Tu aurais pu raconter autre chose. Une autre histoire de ce Que tu faisais avec tes soeurs.

Raconter quoi ? Les sordides moments Que nous avons passé ensemble dans notre petit taudis de Montrouge ? Cela réduirait l'histoire de mes soeurs à un naturalisme pathétique. Mes soeurs méritent mieux Que ça. Mieux qu'une histoire de misère.

Tiens, je vais mettre ici le poème Que j'ai écrit pour ma soeur Jacqueline.

Notre Soeur

    À sa mémoire

mon frère me dit-elle
dans le noir de très loin
écris le poème
que je vais te murmurer

mais il a peur que les mots
ne sortent pas comme il faut

mon frère me dit-elle
de son petit tas de cendres
quand tu traversas l'océan
et que tu as eu le mal de mer
est-ce que tu as été malade
pour moi aussi

mon frère me dit-elle
parmi les feuilles mortes
quand tu es tombé amoureux
pour la première fois
et que tu as ressenti en toi
le grand frisson originel
et que tout s'est mis à tourbillonner
est-ce que tu t'es senti heureux
pour moi aussi

Still on page 7 of your text [77], I pondered this: "Implicit in Federman's dilemma, then, is the thematization of an act which never took place – let's call it the act of dying, dying in the past" –
page 8 [78] has become a huge collage –
you know that this expression – "time immemorial" is used by Beckett a number of times – especially in *The Lost Ones* –
then this "...lampshades indeed have the potential to be the vehicle for illumination" [78] –
yes to illuminate – but also the potential of shading the light –
I think it's in *To Whom It May Concern* that I wrote –
he fears the light that shines through human skin –
I love what you did with the word schmuck –
and I love that first person plural –
in *Double or Nothing* of course
and especially in TTV – federman moinous namredef all speak in the first person through the mouth of Federman [with a capital letter] this is where your reading of TTV touches me the most – no one has really paid attention to the narrative intricacy of this novel – in fact little attention has been given to this novel – it was ignored and is still ignored – sometimes I feel it may be my best novel – but then *Double or Nothing* and *Take It or Leave It* start screaming at me that they are my best – of course the characters in these novels have not read *Return to Manure* and *Chut* –
digression # ? – the other day a young French journalist – quite attractive – concluded an interview we were doing in Paris with this question – *Monsieur Federman quel est votre roman préféré* – and I answered – in English – the one I haven't written yet –
in any case – I often go and read pages of TTV and I am surprised at the things I said in that book –

for instance that the old man was the same age as my father and as myself [and I could have added Sam Beckett too] for indeed the Old Man is all of us – he represents the living-dead and vice versa the dead-living –

page 9 [80] also looks like a collage –

I'll just repeat what I wrote in the margin –

TTV – a danse macabre of pronouns

Wow! I wrote 'wow!' when I discovered that Moinous & Namredef are extradiegetic homodiegetic narrators but at the same time they are also intradiegetic hetero/homodiegetic – Wow! [80]

What a revelation – and nobody knows that – yes they both are, as *The Unnamable* put it of himself – the teller and the told –

you give on page 9 [80-81] the best synopsis of TTV ever given – and so succinctly – you are the first one to notice that Nam and Moimoi are kinds of detectives who have been commissioned to give a report – not unlike Moran in search of Molloy –

it's amazing how present Beckett is in this novel – from the epigraph to the end of the novel where the epigraph is now inscribed into the report –

It's true that their investigation takes place mainly in bars and fancy restaurants – but also in casinos and concert halls and bordello and trains and hotel rooms and....

Best summary ever given of that book –

that's why you are right to say that they always bitch about their plotless existence and its lack of dramatic development – plots are for dead people anyway – and dramatic development only happens in pathetic bestsellers –

page 10 [81–82] has become unreadable, as I filled it with my scribbling in the margins and all over –

the distinction you make between Moinous who always elaborates and Namredef who always interprets were played in the German radio play adapted from this novel by two actors who acted like Gogo & Didi –
N & M as I call them are clowns – I once wrote something asking what ever happened to them – I cannot resist showing it to you – I go get it –

x x x x

Whatever happened to M & N

hey fed ... wake up ... wake up ... we want to ask you something ... you see ... for years we've been wondering whatever happened to M & N after they vanished ... you know ... or as you put it so well yourself then ... after they faded back into your subconscious ... remember ... right there in that old dusty chamber of departure ... after M & N told you what had happened at the spaceport and how the Old Man ... well you know the story ...
yes ... we've often wondered whatever happened to these two old farts... after they vanished... and you fell asleep on the sofa
we would like to know what's doing with them ... that pseudocouple ... as you called them ... echoing Sam's M & C ... when was it ... when was it we last saw them ... 81 ... 82 ... I mean the year of their glorious appearance ... and their pathetic disappearance ... hey ... these two guys didn't last long ... 82 ... wasn't it ... ah what a year it was ... well a good year perhaps for them two bums ... but for us what a stinking year ... one of the worst ... do you remember ...

tell us fed ... have you seen them ... heard from them ... are they still there ... silent ... motionless in your subconscious ... dormant so to speak ... or have they given sign of life ... of reappearance ...
are they still alive or have they already changed tense ... the way these two jokers conducted their life they could outwit death itself ... we wouldn't put it past them to make it to the apocalypse ... just to be able to take a picture of it ...
ah those two bums ... M & N ... they were something ...
hey fed ... do you know anything ... anything of the whereabouts of these two chaos-drunk schmucks ... do you have any idea what they are doing ... and if they are doing anything ... whatever that may be ... do you know where they are doing it ... and how ... and for what purpose ... are they well ... successful ... satisfied ... are they employed ... and do we dare ask ... do we dare ask at the risk of being ridiculous ... are they happy ...
if you know anything fed ... anything at all ... about Ominous & Namredef ... please let us know ... let the rest of us know... there are so many of us who were so fond ... and are still ... of these two clowns ... we urge you to let us know ... we want so much to know ... to hear ... the rest of their story ...

x x x x

that passage you quote from TTV at the bottom of page 9 [80] where they all talk together in the first person – one could call that pure linguistic cacophony –

the director of Indiana U. Press who originally published TTV once wrote me to deplore that the book was not selling very well – and the reason for that – he claimed – was because of the way fit was punctuated – no one has every paid attention to those little comas and wondered what they were doing there ,,,,,,,

it must be irritating to many readers when Federman – the real one – the one with the Capital letter intrudes into the story and explains things to the readers – reveal that M & N are Jewish but that they are only incidental in this story ...

Federman always shows up to undermine everything –

He is incurable –

x x x x

page 12 [84] raises enormous questions.

Amazing, I wrote in the margin, how the Old man often speaks like Federman – for instance when he explains to M & N what the book he wrote is all about – the book that is missing from this book – the voice in the closet –

which, which by the way, was part of the original manuscript of TTV – but the same director of Indiana U. Press refused to publish the book with those 20 unreadable pages – even when I suggested that we do not number these pages so the reader can skip over if he is irritated by these 20 unreadable pages – but the director refused – I would love someday to publish a special edition of the original manuscript – I wish there would also be included beside the text of the voice in the closet – the text I put on my blog recently entitled – "Report from the World Federation of Displaced Writers" – which was one of the chapters of TTV – oh well –

page 12 [84] raised the crucial question of – what if nobody reads – read this story – Federman is so aware of this – that in everything he writes he inscribes a reader or many readers so that there can be an ear or many ears to hear what he is saying – the implied reader

who becomes implicated in the story – as it is said somewhere in TTV – we were all and are still implicated in this sordid affair –
Camelia absolutely brilliant this move to the Federman blog – suppose one could discuss the blog as being part of the Federman oeuvre – another genre – another means of telling the story – the same old story – but in a different mode – a true collage of the old and the used and the abused with the new and yet to be invented – in order to involve all the visitors of the blog into his Jewishness –
I hope your lecture is well received in Romania – maybe the Romanian translation will become a best-seller – and I will be caught with my pants down – confronting the world bareass – as the little boy did in the closet –

    Thank you Camelia for inspiring this delirium –
        – Love, Raymond

Dear Raymond,
One for Moinuous and Namredef, *Checkmate*

Ola, ola, ola, bola, bola, bola. This is not exactly *Parsifal*. Moinous and Namredef like Parsifal. After a lot of singing, there is a lot of dying. "I don't want to go to Dachau," I tell them. I just want the singing. Namredef blurts at me and almost tells me to go fuck myself. "Don't get so worked up," he says, "I'm Jewish too, you know," he further says. "Yeah, sure," I say, and start thinking about what would have happened to Malcolm X's philosophy had he gone to Europe to visit the old concentration camps instead of Mecca. I'm getting twofold vibrations. I wonder if Federman's family had a brief encounter with Max Ernst and Peggy Guggenheim while in there, at that place, the place that Wagner never wanted to mention. Peggy and Max got out. Then Max married Peggy and then he married that American who still wants a lot of colors in her dreams. I see them playing chess in one of Inverarity's framed photographs. Malcolm said: "Be peaceful, be courteous, obey the law, respect everyone; but if someone puts his hand on you, send him to the cemetery." Moinous and Namredef understand this very well, but only when pronounced in another language. They love their reactions to such statements to end with *Halleluiah* and *Amen*, but since they are more cultivated than most Baptists, they like an ending that goes Latin. Thus their favorite is: *nec plus ultra*. Oy, boy! Before the King goes into checkmate, the Queen gives him a kiss under their gazes. M & N approve.

Dear Camelia,
M & N APPROVE 150%
     – Big hug, Raymond

Premembering Time – Archiving Space

Elias: At this point it might just as well be revealed. How did these two meet, Elias and Federman, the curious reader might ask? To begin with, it was a textual, then a virtual, and then an altogether other thing. Federman discovered in 2004, the year of the Karlstad conference, that I had been writing on him. So he wanted my texts. I indulged, of course. Here's a short response to another draft that sparked his imagination. This second *inédit* text reprinted here is meant to perform Federman's concept of "premembering" – remembering the future in the past, or prophesying in an inverse order, to be more precise.

As Federman's text focuses on geographies – we get born, we live, we die – the question that one poses as a premembered act, 'how do we get from there to here, or where do we go from here, or must we absolutely go somewhere?' becomes increasingly significant. In light of such threefoldedness, it makes sense to be reminded, as Federman does, of where the casinos are. What is fascinating about casinos is the fact that they are places suited particularly those to those who like to pose existential questions. Casinos offer a space for the player to eat, make strategic moves, and simply experience being somewhere 'in the meanwhile.' In this transit time, memory can be forgotten, and history can be archived. Here I would advance the claim that what enables writers such as Federman to formulate statements that entangle criticism and fiction, fiction and reality, "really fictitious" discourses with "fictitiously real" fictions, and ultimately biography and autobiography, is 'the meanwhile.' Meanwhile it is then. Thus we quote by stealing through permission:

Federman: I just made an incredible discovery.
I'm sitting at the kitchen table eating a sandwich of paté with french *cornichons au vinaigre et* drinking *un verre de cidre,* and while eating I'm reading an article I just got from Camelia Elias – a professor of English at the University of Aalborg in Denmark. The article is called "H(a)unting Potentialities in Federman's Frenzies." So I'm reading while chewing my sandwich, and on page 2, I read this passage from *Take It or Leave It* which Camelia is quoting to illustrate

what would have happened if Federman had not left himself open to other possibilities. I am reading, reading that passage aloud to bring it back to life.

> Take my case for instance. What do you think I would be today if it were not for Hitler? Do you know what I would be today? I mean if nothing had happened. No war, no occupation, no collaboration, no deportation, no extermination – no Holocaust.

I stop reading a moment and mumble to myself. Aloud. Federman you're a fucking good writer. Look at that style. That succession of words that rime and how they explode after the little hesitation of the – into the Holocaust. I smile and continue reading aloud. This time with a Parisian accent.

> Yes, do you know what I would be today? A tailor. A little Jewish tailor slaving in a tailor shop on *Boulevard des Italiens* in Paris...

I stop reading and repeat *Boulevard des Italiens*. And suddenly it hits me. Everybody these days, in France, in Germany, and other places in the world, including Denmark now, is trying to replace Federman's story with history in order to find out who he is, and why he writes the way he does.

But as I stop and repeat *Boulevard des Italiens*, it comes to me that it is not with history but with geography that one will understand who federman is and why he writes the way he does.

Throughout his fiction – his stories – Federman has given a quantity of addresses and geographical locations. Specific addresses. Street names. Places in cities and in the countryside. Villages. Town. Cities. Churches & monuments. Countries. And even space colonies. And no one has ever paid attention to these geographical indications. These landmarks. There lies the real story, in those addresses, those locations.

Why, one should ask, did Federman decide, when he wrote that passage, that he would have ended at a little Jewish tailor on *Boulevard des Italiens*? Why there and not somewhere else in Paris? What does *Boulevard des Italiens* signify for Federman? We know what *4 rue Louis Roland* means. He has often enough given his home address in *Montrouge* for those who might be interested to see where it all started. I mean the story.

So many countries are mentioned in Federman's fiction. So many cities. Streets. Locations. And so many casinos too, one should not forget.

So, there, I am finishing my sandwich when this hits me. I immediately call Larry McCaffery to explain all this to him. I even read him the passage from TIOLI. And Larry, as always when I throw a mad idea at him, says it's terrific, and so I tell Larry to sit his ass in front of his computer and start writing an article called "Federman's Geography."

And Larry says he will. But can I trust him? Maybe I should write "Federman's Geography" myself. This would save Larry, or whoever picks on the idea, a lot of travel expenses, because by necessity whoever writes "Federman's Geography" would have to travel to all these place to find the facts of that specific location. I know exactly why such and such addresses were given. Or such places in a city. For instance the Ritz Hôtel where Federman put Aunt Rachel when she came to Paris from Senegal. Why the Ritz? Why not the George Cinq? These are delicate questions that only Federman can answer.

But will he tell us? That remains the mystery of Federman's fiction.

www.ingramcontent.com/pod-product-compliance
Lightning Source LLC
Chambersburg PA
CBHW022015160426
43197CB00007B/440